YORK

General Editor:
of Stirling) & F
University of Beirut)

James Joyce

A PORTRAIT OF THE ARTIST AS A YOUNG MAN

Notes by Harry Blamires
MA (OXFORD)
Former Head of the English Department,
King Alfred's College, Winchester

LONGMAN
YORK PRESS

YORK PRESS
Immeuble Esseily, Place Riad Solh, Beirut.

LONGMAN GROUP UK LIMITED
Longman House,
Burnt Mill,
Harlow,
Essex

© Librairie du Liban 1984

*All rights reserved; no part of this publication may be reproduced, stored
in a retrieval system, or transmitted in any form or by any means,
electronic, mechanical, photocopying, recording, or otherwise, without the
prior written permission of the copyright owner.*

First published 1984
Third impression 1988

ISBN 0-582-03088-9

Produced by Longman Group (FE) Ltd
Printed in Hong Kong

Contents

Contents

Part 1

Introduction

James Joyce

James Joyce was born in 1882 in Rathgar, Dublin. He was the eldest to survive in a family of four boys and six girls. His father, John Joyce, had inherited property in his home town, Cork, and was Collector of Rates for Dublin at the time of James's birth. It was an undemanding, well-paid post, but John Joyce was a reckless spender and a heavy drinker, and he had begun to mortgage his Cork properties as early as 1881. As his family grew in number, so did the mortgages. In 1892 his post was abolished and he was pensioned off at the age of forty-two. Thereafter a rapid decline in the family fortunes set in. James had been sent to Clongowes Wood College, a highly thought-of Jesuit school in County Kildare, but he was withdrawn in 1891 after three years there. He spent some time at a Christian Brothers' school until Father Conmee, former rector of Clongowes, who knew him as a very promising pupil, kindly arranged for him to have a free place at Belvedere College, the Jesuit school in Dublin.

At first Joyce worked well at Belvedere: he won exhibitions in annual examinations and he was noted for his piety, becoming head of the Sodality of the Blessed Virgin Mary in 1896. However, it appears that in that same year, at the age of fourteen, he met a prostitute one night and had his first sexual experience. Not long afterwards, in a school retreat conducted by Father James A. Cullen at the end of November and the beginning of December 1896, Joyce was deeply stirred by guilt feelings, went to confession, and for some months tried seriously to live a life of piety. But his faith then began to disintegrate. He rejected the suggestion that he should become a priest, and he became more careless in his studies.

Joyce proceeded to University College, Dublin, in 1898, where he studied English, French and Italian, and took his BA degree in 1902. Throughout his Belvedere days and his university days the home situation was deteriorating. John Joyce, boisterous, garrulous, and irresponsible as ever, was drinking and boasting the family into poverty. He moved the family rapidly from house to house to escape rent-hungry landlords, having sometimes first burned the house banisters for firewood. He was cruel to his wife and once when drunk tried to strangle her. Joyce's brother, Stanislaus, understandably detested him: but

Joyce never lost his queer sympathy for him, and relished his wit, his racy turns of phrase, his powers of mimicry, his fine tenor voice, and his laughably irrepressible refusal to face facts.

Joyce wrote an article on Ibsen which was published in the *Fortnightly Review* in 1900 and actually drew a favourable comment from Ibsen himself. With the twelve guineas he was paid for it he took his father on a brief trip to London. Anxious to be a writer, he tried his hand at a play, wrote poems, and made contact with influential literary figures such as George Russell, W.B. Yeats, and Lady Gregory. Thinking at this time of taking up a medical career, and finding that he would be unable to raise the money to study medicine in Dublin, he planned to do so in Paris and to make money by teaching English, and he left Dublin in December 1902. After a brief trip home at Christmas, he returned to Paris in January 1903, but was called back to Dublin by telegram in April because his mother was dying of cancer. At Easter she begged him to go to confession and take communion, but he refused. She died in August 1903.

During the subsequent twelve months Joyce did some book-reviewing, began work on his autobiographical novel, *Stephen Hero*, considered the possibility of a singing career and had some singing lessons, taught briefly in a school at Dalkey, had some short stories printed in a magazine, the *Irish Homestead*, and in June 1904 met Nora Barnacle, a girl from Galway, with whom he fell in love. The two of them left together for the Continent in October.

Thereafter Joyce lived the life of an exile. He supported his family by teaching English in Trieste, in Zurich, and back again in Trieste. The patronage of Harriet Weaver and others eventually enabled him to be a full-time writer, and the family lived in Paris from 1920 until the Second World War drove them back to Zurich. The Joyces had two children, Giorgio and Lucia. Joyce and Nora formalised their relationship by marrying in 1931. In 1941 Joyce died, of a perforated ulcer, in Zurich.

Joyce inherited some of his father's weaknesses, notably his taste for alcohol and his irresponsibility with money; but he was devoted to his work and to his family. He suffered from very bad eyesight and had several operations on his eyes. Another worry was the worsening schizophrenia of his daughter, Lucia, who was to die in a mental hospital in Northampton in 1982.

Joyce's short stories of Dublin characters, *Dubliners*, was published in 1914, and *A Portrait of the Artist* followed two years later. His masterpiece, *Ulysses*, on which he spent seven years, came out in 1922. This story of Dublin life on one June day in 1904 presents again the Stephen Dedalus of *A Portrait* after his return from France and his mother's death, but the hero of the book is Leopold Bloom, a Jewish advertising agent, whose activities in Dublin on the crucial day, together with reflections on his past history, are in many respects parallel with the adventures of Ulysses in Homer's epic poem, the *Odyssey*. *Ulysses* is a big book. It compresses a vast panorama of life into its pages and exploits an elaborate system of symbols to make its situations applicable to people anywhere. The achievement inspired Joyce to an even longer and more ambitious work, *Finnegans Wake* (1937). The far-reaching experiments with language which he made in this work render it extremely difficult to read.

Historical and cultural background

The Act of Union which made Ireland part of the United Kingdom and abolished the separate Irish Parliament in Dublin was passed in 1800. Throughout the nineteenth century various movements developed which gave expression to the demands of the Irish for greater control of their own affairs at home. British rule had given to Ireland not only an Anglo-Irish aristocracy of landowners but also a Protestant Church of Ireland of which the ruling minority tended to be members. Thus the Roman Catholic Church was by and large the Church of the peasantry and of the majority of the Irish population. In the last decades of the nineteenth century there was a very complex relationship between the numerous movements in which the desire for a distinctive Irish identity expressed itself. There were movements for land reform which were designed to improve the lot of the Irish peasantry, movements for Home Rule in an Irish parliament, movements for total independence from Great Britain and the setting up of a republic, movements to revive Gaelic as the national language, and movements to revitalise Irish literature in English from historic and legendary Irish sources. An Irishman might be a keen advocate of one or more of these causes and yet be at loggerheads with a fellow-Irishman who supported another of these causes. The possibilities for argument and strife among the Irish themselves were vast. Charles Stewart Parnell (1846–91) was the great advocate of parliamentary Home Rule for Ireland. Michael Davitt (1846–1906) was an advocate of land reform. The attempts of the British Prime Minister, W.E. Gladstone (1809–98), to establish Home Rule in Ireland were defeated at Westminster in 1886 and 1892 during Joyce's childhood and youth.

The story of Parnell's downfall casts a shadow over *A Portrait*. It illustrates how complicated was the relationship between different factions of nationalistic Irishmen. Parnell's work in the Land League for securing land-ownership for tenant farmers and his leadership of the Home Rule Party as a Member of Parliament at Westminster gained him immense popularity at home and the title of 'uncrowned king of Ireland'. When, in 1890, he was cited as co-respondent in a divorce case by the husband of Kitty O'Shea, his mistress, most of his party deserted him and the Catholic clergy turned against him. He died soon after in 1891, and intense bitterness was felt by those of his supporters who had remained loyal to him. They regarded him as a hero who had been treacherously betrayed, and their anger was acute and long-lasting. The grip of the Roman Catholic Church on the mass of the Irish was a powerful one. The Anglo-Irish ascendancy was largely Protestant, and nationalistic movements tended to appeal to Catholics though Parnell himself was a Protestant landowner. The Catholic Church's moral condemnation of Parnell was typical of what often happened at crucial turning-points in Irish political history. Loyalties were confused. The Church which was a bulwark of Irishness helped to destroy Ireland's most popular nationalist leader.

Joyce was brought up in a Catholic family with a pious mother and a father who was an enthusiastic Home-Ruler and supporter of Parnell. John Joyce's anti-clericalism was not shared by his wife nor by 'Dante' Conway, a widow who was brought into the Joyce household to be a governess ('Dante' was a childish corruption of 'Aunty'). She was a fierce partisan of the clergy. Dante's influence on the child James is made evident in *A Portrait*. In earlier life she had been narrowly saved from entering an American convent by inheriting a fortune from her brother. Coming back to Ireland, she married a man who worked in the Bank of Ireland, and soon after he absconded to South America with her cash. An educated woman, she was understandably soured by her experience.

Joyce's education was well looked after by the Jesuits and it was logical that, as an academically promising student, he should go to University College. The main and most prestigious university institution in Ireland was Trinity College, Dublin, originally founded by Queen Elizabeth I and provided with splendid buildings in the eighteenth century. Its Anglican tradition and its association with the Anglo-Irish ascendancy did not make it natural for families such as the Joyces to aspire to it. There was an attempt in the nineteenth century to provide university education in Ireland on a non-sectarian basis, and 'Queen's Colleges' were founded in Belfast, Galway, and Cork. John Joyce himself was a student at Queen's College, Cork. But the Irish Catholics were opposed to inter-denominational institutions and to purely secular education, and a Catholic University of Ireland was founded in Dublin in 1852. This became University College. In Joyce's time the college was in St Stephen's Green.

Joyce's short stories, *Dubliners*, presented the people of Dublin as given to talk, sentimentality, and acquiescence rather than to decisive action. Yet at the turn of the century Dublin was in fact astir with new ideas and enthusiasm in the cultural field. There was a revival of

interest in the Gaelic language and there was also a movement to give
Irish literature in English a native vitality that would be the mainspring
of the campaign for political independence. At the same time enthusi-
asts were working for the establishment of an Irish National Theatre in
Dublin. *A Portrait* refers to the first performance of W.B. Yeats's
(1865–1939) play, *The Countess Cathleen*, in the Antient Concert
Rooms in 1899, the first venture of what was called the Irish Literary
Theatre. Joyce himself was present on this occasion and sympathised
with Yeats when the play provoked a clash with upholders of Catholic
orthodoxy. In 1904, the year Joyce left Dublin for good, the first per-
formances were given in the Abbey Theatre of plays by Yeats and Lady
(Augusta) Gregory (1852–1932). Other names associated with the Irish
literary movement at this time were George Moore (1852–1933), the
novelist, and John Millington Synge (1871–1909), the dramatist.

Joyce's inability to share the enthusiasms of these various writers,
like his detachment from the movement to popularise the Irish language, was partly due to his rejection of Irish cultural insularity. His
early enthusiasm for the Norwegian dramatist Henrik Ibsen (1828–
1906) shows how European his interests were. His grounding in English
literature made him scornful of people who tried to push the Gaelic
language by denigrating English. His sense of the wastefulness and
crudity of violence made the mentality of the extreme nationalists
repellent to him.

These were some of the complex reasons behind the dissatisfaction
with Ireland which led Joyce to exile. There were more personal motives
too. The young James Joyce had his share of vanity and pride. He felt
he had a claim on the support and patronage of established writers
which he did not always receive. He could be prickly, even uncouth,
when he thought he was being patronised or not given his due. His poverty did not help to make him a socially presentable figure and some of
his personal habits did not help either. He was aided in various ways by
Lady Gregory, Yeats, and A.E. (pen-name of George Russell, 1867–
1938, the highly influential poet and editor), but he was acutely sensitive to real or imagined instances of cold-shouldering. But quite apart
from all these reasons, no doubt forsaking Ireland must have seemed
absolutely essential to a young man who wished to dedicate himself to
writing and whose family situation was such that not even the most stren-
uous labours, nor the most saintly patience and sympathy, could rescue
the home from squalor and disorder. John Joyce had once screamed
drunkenly at his dying wife, 'Die, and be damned to you!'

The great irony of Joyce's literary achievement is that the man who
forsook Ireland with the conscious determination to work in exile
never wrote anything that did not focus lovingly as well as critically on
Dublin and its inhabitants.

There is a story told on good authority that when *Stephen Hero*, the first version of Joyce's autobiographical novel, was rejected by a publisher, Joyce threw it on the fire and Nora Joyce rescued much of it. In fact, none of the surviving manuscript shows any trace of such an adventure. It was a long manuscript of some nine hundred pages, and the pages that survived began at page 519. Thus they focus on Stephen's years as a university student and match roughly the last quarter of *A Portrait*. They were edited by Theodore Spencer and published in 1944. A revised edition, containing some newly discovered fragments, was published in 1956, edited by John J. Slocum and Herbert Cahoon. These publications thus saw the light only several decades after *A Portrait*.

It is easy to understand why the manuscript of *Stephen Hero* failed to find a publisher. By comparison with *A Portrait* its style is more direct and its presentation of Stephen's mental development more detailed. Moreover its descriptions of certain episodes that are only obliquely touched upon in *A Portrait*, or even ignored there, are evocatively full. Nevertheless the text of *Stephen Hero* is in general too diffuse and its tone too claustrophobic and self-centred for the book to have the appeal of its successor. It is, of course, fascinating to compare *Stephen Hero* with the last section of *A Portrait* and to see how Joyce gained in artistry—in judicious selectivity, in cultivating skilfully oblique narration, and in the gift for twining threads of Stephen's varied experience into a rich pattern.

A note on the text

A Portrait of the Artist as a Young Man was first published in instalments in the London journal, *The Egoist*, between 1914 and 1915. It was first published in book form by W.B. Huebsch in New York in 1916, and an English edition, published by The Egoist Ltd, followed in London in 1917. Chester G. Anderson edited *A Portrait of the Artist as a Young Man* in the Viking Critical Editions, New York, 1967. Editions currently available are that from Heinemann Educational, London, 1979, and the Panther paperback, Granada, London, 1977.

Part 2

Summaries
of A PORTRAIT OF THE
ARTIST AS A YOUNG MAN

A general summary

A Portrait of the Artist as a Young Man traces the growth and development of Stephen Dedalus from infancy to young manhood. His story runs parallel to that of Joyce himself in some respects but differs in others. Stephen's infancy is passed at home with his father and mother and a governess he calls 'Dante'. He is sent at the age of six to Clongowes Wood College, a Jesuit Boarding School, where he is sometimes bullied by other boys and on one occasion punished unjustly by a cruel schoolmaster. His father is a feckless fellow who talks too much and drinks too much, and there is a steady decline in the family fortunes. Stephen is withdrawn from Clongowes in consequence and the family moves from a comfortable suburban house to a bare and cheerless one in Dublin. A friendly priest, however, arranges for Stephen to get a free place at Belvedere, a Jesuit day school in the city.

Much of Stephen's story concerns his sexual and artistic development. In all respects he gradually separates himself from his own family. He becomes totally disillusioned with his father during a visit to the latter's home town of Cork. He reads Romantic literature which stirs in him an imaginative interest in girls, but he is timid and unresponsive when actually in close company with Emma Clery, a girl who attracts him. At school he is clever and a leader, but is awkwardly conscious of his queer position as the son of a parent who cannot afford the fees. His various frustrations come to a head one night when he meets a prostitute in the street and she takes him to her room to initiative him into sex.

Stephen has been an obedient young Catholic and the new habit of visiting brothels makes him morally uncomfortable. He attends a school retreat where the conductor's hell-fire sermons move him to anguished self-disgust and terrified remorse. He goes to confession, is absolved, and finds peace again. Now for a time he endeavours to lead a life of exemplary piety, and it is suggested to him that he might himself have a vocation to the priesthood, but an inner conviction tells him that his vocation is to become a creative writer rather than to enter into the orderly, inhibiting routines of the Church.

Stephen goes to University College, Dublin. He does not take his official courses very seriously but he works thoughtfully at his own philosophical interests and hammers out an aesthetic theory to inspire him in his future career. As a student he makes friends with a number of contemporaries, but he cannot share the enthusiasm of some of them for political activism or Irish nationalism, and he has lost his faith in the Church. Emma can still inspire him to write romantic poetry, but he is incurably distrustful of her. Gradually he senses his isolation from home, Church, and native country and opts for exile.

Detailed summaries

NOTE: *A Portrait of the Artist as a Young Man* is divided by Joyce into five numbered chapters. Each of these chapters is sub-divided into sections which are not numbered: the breaks between them are marked in some editions by asterisks. The sub-divisions are here numbered and are called 'Sections'.

Chapter 1, Section i

The book opens with Stephen's memories of his infancy. He recalls a bedtime story his father used to tell him, and how his father's hairy face and his monocle distinguished him from his mother. He recalls too the first song he tried lispingly to sing. Then come memories of bedtime and bed-wetting. The immediate relief and cosy warmth occasioned by wetting the bed was quickly cancelled out by cold and discomfort. Mother is remembered for her nice smell and her piano tunes. The family circle also included Uncle Charles and Dante. The neighbours, the Vances, had a daughter Eileen with whom he played. The section ends with Stephen hiding under the table after being naughty, while his mother and Dante urge him to apologise.

COMMENTARY: The memories of infancy are vivid but disconnected impressions that tumble back through the mind haphazardly, yet are all significant. The little boy of the story was Stephen himself setting out on the road of life and meeting the animal which is the symbol of Ireland. The song he learned was 'Lily Dale', and the chorus actually goes: 'Now the wild rose blossoms/O'er her little green grave'. The bed-wetting memory is a child's early experience of how seizing pleasure may quickly lead to disillusionment. Though Stephen is at the centre of a friendly, protective family circle, the association of Dante's brushes with rival political factions hints at public division in the background. A major theme is introduced in the contrast between the dream of marrying the girl across the way and having to shrink guiltily from the demand to conform. Stephen's position under the table foreshadows future demands for repentance and threats of hell-fire.

NOTES AND GLOSSARY:

lemon platt: lemon-flavoured sticks of barley sugar
O, the green wothe botheth: the child's attempt to sing 'O, the green rose blossoms' (should be 'wild rose')
press: cupboard
Michael Davitt: (1846–1906) Irish nationalist leader who struggled for the rights of the oppressed peasantry against the landlords. At first a great supporter of Parnell, he later diverged from him in policy and opposed him after the scandal
Parnell: Charles Stewart Parnell (1846–91). See 'Historical and cultural background' in Part 1, above
Pull out his eyes: there was a children's hymn about the punishment of the wicked: 'The ravens shall pick out his eyes/ And eagles eat the same' (based on the Bible, *Proverbs*, 30: 17)

Chapter 1, Section ii

Some years have passed. Stephen is now at Clongowes Wood College, County Kildare. He is on the school playing-field. His companions are playing football, but he is trying to avoid notice, for he feels small and weak and is conscious of his defective eyesight. He recalls how his parents waved good-bye to him and looks forward to ticking off another day of term after supper (seventy-six instead of seventy-seven days now to go before the holidays).

By contrast with the cold outside, the lighted castle looks attractive and its romantic historical associations stir his imagination. He is shivering because the bully Wells shouldered him into the cold slimy water of the square ditch. Thoughts of the home fireside at teatime impinge before the scene shifts to a mathematics lesson under Father Arnall, then to the refectory, where Stephen finds that he cannot eat, and sits disconsolately, elbows on table, covering and uncovering his ears so that the noise of the refectory is like that of a train roaring and quietening as it runs in and out of tunnels. A little later, isolated in the playroom, he is again mocked by Wells.

When the bell rings he goes to the study hall and he ticks the day off inside the lid of his desk. He takes out a geography text-book with a picture of the world floating in clouds. He has written his name in the book and his school address in the universe. The mystery of the universe and its immensity baffle him. He feels very small in it—and in the Clongowes world too. Cold and tired, he thinks longingly of bed as the bell calls the boys to night prayers in chapel.

In the dormitory afterwards he undresses, prays for the family at home, and climbs into bed. Thoughts of the building's legendary ghosts come frighteningly to mind, but are eventually replaced by dreams of going home. Next morning he wakes to the noise of curtains being drawn and water poured into basins as boys get up, but Stephen lies hot and limp, and makes only a feeble attempt to dress. Fleming sees that he is ill and tells him to get back into bed. The prefect comes to check that he is really sick, before ordering him off to the infirmary.

Brother Michael receives him there. Stephen wonders whether his parents have been informed that he is sick and imagines a letter he might write to tell them. The thought that he might die conjures up pictures of how the school would hold a requiem mass for him and bury him. He recalls a funereal verse, and its sad poetic phrases move him almost to tears.

The fellow-occupant of the sick-room asks Brother Michael, who is going out for a time, to be sure to come back with the day's news, and Stephen's mind turns to sensational items of news, accidents, shipwrecks, and the like. There is talk with the fellow-invalid, Athy, about their respective names and their fathers. Daylight fades and the firelight flickers on the walls. It appears that time has passed and that Brother Michael has indeed brought the latest news for, in Stephen's delirious sickness, talk of Parnell's death merges with the thoughts of death and disaster that have been preoccupying him.

COMMENTARY: The reader is kept in touch with the outer scene only fitfully. For the most part we follow Stephen's thoughts, and they are those of someone sickening for a chill. The first separation from home at Clongowes is a move from the warmth and cosiness of the family circle to a world of cold, discomfort, and harassment by other boys. They touch a raw nerve when they want to know what his father is, for disillusionment with his father is to become a crucial theme. The recurring contrast between cold and hot is merged with the contrast between white and red. The two teams into which Stephen's form is divided for competitions are called 'York' and 'Lancaster', referring to the English Wars of the Roses, the civil wars of the fifteenth century, a struggle for supremacy between the rival houses of York and Lancaster in which Yorkists wore white roses and Lancastrians wore red roses as symbols of their allegiances. In the alternate cold and hot of Stephen's chill white and red become symbols of sickness as well as of English civil strife. You cannot have a 'green rose', which would blend Ireland's colour with the English royal flower. But Stephen's dream of a happy Christmas at home blends 'holly and ivy, green and red' together. Irish green and English red are even twined 'round the old portraits on the walls', seeming to obliterate disharmony. The same dream of fulfilment transforms Stephen's father into something higher even than a magistrate—a marshal.

In the real world at Clongowes things are different. Stephen finds himself jeered at when he admits that he kisses his mother at bedtime and jeered at again when he denies that he kisses her. The difficulty of being accepted in a world where such unjust conditions obtain produces a mental confusion that matches the physical confusion of hot and cold.

The future artist is already fascinated by historical associations, by poetry, and by words generally. The five senses, already shown as awakening in Section i, are all developing in response to the world around him—the touch of cold water, the smell of old peasants, the sound of boys in the refectory. Stephen is consciously becoming a person for whom thinking can bring pleasure, and he is becoming aware of his place in a vast universe.

His delirious dream prefigures the arrival home of Parnell's body. Parnell died in England and his body was brought over to Kingstown harbour, south of Dublin before burial at Glasnevin Cemetery, north of Dublin.

NOTES AND GLOSSARY:

prefects:	schoolmasters who had been given special responsibilities
third line:	the under-thirteens at Clongowes (lower line: thirteen to fifteen years, higher line: fifteen years and over)
greaves in his number:	shin-pads in his individual (numbered) locker
the castle:	Clongowes Wood College had a restored medieval castle in its precincts
Hamilton Rowan:	Archibald Hamilton Rowan (1751–1834) was a supporter of Wolfe Tone, the eighteenth-century Dublin nationalist who tried to unite Irishmen against Britain. Hamilton was supposed to have fled to the castle when convicted of sedition in 1794. While pursuing soldiers were shooting bullets into the door, he threw his hat from a window into the garden to send them on a false trail. He is sometimes confused with Sir William Rowan Hamilton (1805–65) the distinguished Irish mathematician, inventor of quaternions, and Irish Astronomer Royal
haha:	a steep bank designed to keep cattle out of a garden; the hat would be conspicuous on it
the square ditch:	the 'square' is the boys' lavatories, with urinal and 'closets'. The ditch is an open drain carrying the urinal water
hacking chestnut:	his prize conker

suck: (*slang*) someone's favourite who 'sucks up' to the person in question

wax: (*slang*) rage

elements: Stephen is in the Class of Elements, a lower ('third line') form concentrating on basic subjects

third of grammar: the class above Stephen's

fellows in poetry and rhetoric: boys in the two 'higher line' forms

Hayfoot! Strawfoot!: Left, Right (Hay and straw were tied to the feet of rural recruits who might not master the distinction between left and right)

Chapter 1, Section iii

Stephen is at home for the much longed-for Christmas celebrations. Uncle Charles, somewhat neglected, sits over by the window. Mr Dedalus and Mr Casey are sitting by the fire and enjoying a glass of whisky when dinner is brought in.

All is seemingly harmonious until a piece of gossip is repeated about a Catholic who has criticised his parish priest for bringing politics into the pulpit. Dante is outraged at the man's effrontery, while Mr Dedalus and Mr Casey, both devoted to Parnell, resent the Church's part in destroying him. Dante launches into a diatribe against those who lack respect for the clergy, and Mr Dedalus and Mr Casey respond with a crude outburst of anti-clericalism.

Mr Casey then tells the story of one of Parnell's last meetings at which a drunken old woman called Kitty O'Shea an unrepeatable name (presumably a 'whore'), and he spat a volley of tobacco juice into her face. Mr Dedalus and he rock with laughter. Dante is angry. Meanwhile Stephen is confused. He recalls an occasion when a policeman called at their house one night and Mr Casey went off by car. He knows his father's devotion to Parnell and Ireland, but he has also seen Dante hit a man on the head with her umbrella for taking off his hat for 'God save the Queen'.

All restraint has gone. Mr Dedalus laments that the Irish are 'priest-ridden' while Dante calls Parnell a 'traitor'. Mr Casey speaks of earlier betrayals of Ireland by the clergy, while Dante declares that the clergy are always right. Amid shouts of mutual abuse she departs in a quivering rage, and Mr Dedalus sobs, 'Poor Parnell'.

COMMENTARY: This section is perhaps the most conventionally designed part of the book. It is a skilfully shaped episode, dramatic in presentation, with a neatly controlled tension and a fine climax. In itself it might make a first-rate short story. Mr Casey is a delightful study. He shares a silent joke with Stephen by tapping the swollen gland in his neck and smiling. He used to explain the mystery of the swelling to little Stephen by saying he kept a purse of silver in his throat and by making an appropriate noise. He joked too about his three cramped fingers, damaged by picking oakum in gaol. They were damaged 'making a birthday present for Queen Victoria', he used to say.

Mr Dedalus is a generous host, ready with jokes and mimicry, and quick with fluent vituperation when roused. He is genuinely attached to Parnell (who was a Protestant), while Dante is a passionate partisan of the Catholic clergy. The situation would have been in real life an explosive one.

For Stephen the scene is at first all warmth and cosiness. Joyce's colour symbolism underlines the sense of harmony: there is a red fire, green ivy, red holly, and a green flag on the cake. Clongowes, where 'turkey' is a name for the pandybat, is far away. But he cannot reconcile the quiet, lovable Mr Casey's view of the priests with Dante's. By the end of the episode he is terrified. The pressures of conflict in home, Church, and country have impinged on the family scene to turn a party that promised cheerfulness into a chaos of bitterness.

It is on record that Eileen Vance, by then a married woman in Canada, recalled over fifty years later that the row at the Joyce's Christmas party in 1891 could be heard right across the street. Joyce, however, has not followed the chronology of his own life story exactly. The party here comes at the end of Stephen's first term at Clongowes and Joyce's first term there ended in December 1888, three years before Parnell's death.

NOTES AND GLOSSARY:

Mr Casey: his real name was John Kelly. He had been in prison several times for his involvement in nationalist activities. He was a welcome guest at the Joyces' home. It is true that a policeman called unofficially one night to warn that a warrant would be served on Kelly next morning; so he got away by night

the real Ally Daly: (*slang*) first-class

pandybat: a leather strap strengthened with bone, used for corporal punishment

Woe be to the man: Dante is quoting the Bible, Luke 17: 1−2

Billy with the lip: Archbishop Walsh of Dublin

tub of guts up in Armagh: Archbishop Logue of Armagh

Lord Leitrim's coachman: Lord Leitrim, English landowner in Ireland, was murdered in 1877, though his coachman tried to save him

Touch them not: Dante is getting mixed up. These are not Christ's words but occur in the Bible, Zechariah 2: 8−9

Bishop Lanigan: Bishop of Ossory. He presented a complimentary address to the Lord Lieutenant on the occasion of the Union

Marquess Corwallis: he became Lord Lieutenant and Commander-in-Chief in Ireland in 1798. Pitt, the British Prime Minister, promised Catholics that full emancipation would follow from having a united parliament. This won Catholic support for the Union, but George III refused his royal assent to emancipation in 1801. The Emancipation Bill was passed by parliament in 1829

the fenian movement: the Irish republican movement

Terence Bellew MacManus: (1823–60) revolutionary Irish patriot, tried for treason, transported for life, died in poverty in America. His ashes were brought home and buried in Dublin with a nationalist demonstration which Cardinal Cullen opposed

---

Chapter 1, Section iv

Stephen is back at school. Boys are talking excitedly together about five of their fellows now in disgrace. One story is that they ran away, having stolen money from the rector's room; another story is that they stole altar wine from the sacristy. Stephen is shocked at the enormity of such a crime. He cannot see properly because the day before a boy on a bicycle knocked him down, breaking his glasses. Athy has a third version of why the disgraced boys ran off. They were caught 'smugging' in the lavatories, which seems to mean that they were masturbating together. Stephen is mystified. There is talk of the punishments in store for the offenders and possibly for everybody.

The boys are called in from the playground. In the writing lesson Stephen sits with arms folded. He has been excused work because he cannot see. Father Arnall comes in for the Latin lesson, returns their exercises with his criticisms, and tests the boys with some questions. Fleming says the Latin noun *mare* ('the sea') has no plural and is ordered to kneel in the middle of the class. Soon afterwards Father Dolan, the prefect of studies, comes in with his cane, ready to punish any idlers. Fleming is noticed and duly caned. Then Father Dolan pounces on Stephen because he is not writing. He ignores Father Arnall's explanation of the matter and canes Stephen who is overwhelmed by the injustice of it.

After the lesson the other boys advise him to go to the rector and complain. Deeply humiliated, Stephen cannot eat his supper and resolves to do what they suggest. He is not absolutely sure that he will find justice, but he summons up his courage at the end of the meal and makes for the rector's room. As he moves along the gallery towards it he is aware (though he cannot see properly) of the portraits of saints and great men hanging on the walls.

The rector receives him kindly and he makes his complaint. When Father Conmee suggests that Father Dolan must have made a mistake, Stephen boldly insists that it was not so. The rector promises to speak to Father Dolan himself and Stephen is overcome with gratitude. He races back downstairs and out into the open, where the other boys lock hands together and raise him aloft in triumph.

COMMENTARY: In this, unlike the previous section, attention is focused on Stephen almost from first to last. His imagination is stirred by the wickedness of stealing altar wine. His mind turns to the holiness of the sacristy where he himself has been vested as boat-bearer for a solemn procession to an altar in the wood. Later his over-inventive imagination elaborates the crime into the theft of a monstrance. His mind is thrilled to toy with the notion of a sin so grave as stealing the receptacle into which God himself is placed. The fact that no such sin has been committed or discussed adds spice to Joyce's gentle mockery of Stephen.

In another direction his imagination brings a new insight. 'Lady' Boyle's white hands remind him of Eileen's. The fact that they are like ivory makes sense of the litany of the Virgin Mary in which she is called *Tower of Ivory*. At the Christmas party the same idea occurred to him: it refutes the Protestant notion that a woman could not be a *Tower of Ivory*. *House of Gold* is equally understandable in the litany of the Virgin Mary, for Eileen's hair is gold in the sunlight. The link between idealisation of the Virgin Mary and youthful responsiveness to the opposite sex is clear. An undercurrent of unconscious sexual association also seems to link the memory of how Eileen once put her hand in his pocket with the strange doings of the offenders in the school lavatory.

It is in relation to his schoolmasters and their behaviour that Stephen's mental development is most marked in this section. For instance, they get angry and anger is a sin. Perhaps Father Arnall only pretends to be angry, Stephen thinks. Or perhaps a priest is allowed to be angry when dealing with idle boys. Thus Stephen probes the morality of priests, and the issue becomes more than a matter of mere theory when Father Dolan sweeps in. A thoroughly unpleasant bully, he relishes his role as persecutor. Stephen's burning pain, unjustly inflicted, is a practical revelation on the very subject he has pondered. A priest can be an awful brute. So it is that, with a little encouragement from other boys, he foresees himself protesting and being vindicated like great heroes of history.

The young artist strikes his blow against injustice and is seemingly victorious. In a final stroke of gentle irony, Joyce shows him modest and magnanimous in victory—determined not to show pride before Father Dolan but to be especially submissive.

NOTES AND GLOSSARY:

fecked:	(*slang*) stolen
scut:	(*slang*) ran away
sacristy:	a room set aside for keeping vessels and vestments used in worship
boatbearer, censer:	the censer holds burning charcoal on to which incense is thrown. A server holds the censer which hangs by chains so that it can be swung and will give off clouds of sweet-smelling smoke. The boatbearer walks beside the server, carrying a boat-shaped vessel containing grains of incense for replenishing the censer
prof:	(*slang*) captain
football fifteen:	Irish rugby football had fifteen men a side
Balbus was building a wall:	a typical sentence for translation into Latin in an elementary Latin text-book
The Calico Belly:	Julius Caesar's (100−44BC) work, often used in schools, was his *History of the Gallic War*, the Latin title of which is *De Bello Gallico*
ferulae:	(*Latin*) 'whips' or 'rods'
monstrance:	an ornamental vessel, often made of gold, in which the consecrated bread used in the Mass may be shown to the congregation for veneration. It is placed on the altar amid flowers and candles for the service of Benediction
theme:	an essay (this was a term generally used in Jesuit schools)
minister, rector, provincial, general:	different grades in the Jesuit hierarchy
The senate and the Roman people:	translation of the Latin formula used to introduce official decrees
Lent:	season of forty days' fasting before Easter
Richmal Magnall's Questions:	(should be 'Mangnall') an elementary English text-book in history
Peter Parley's Tales about Greece and Rome:	two popular American text-books
Ignatius Loyola:	(1491−1556) founder of the Jesuits, or Society of Jesus. He is pointing to an open book in the portrait because the story is that, nobly born, he was recuperating after receiving a wound in battle and reading the lives of Christ and of the saints when he decided to change his life and become a soldier of Christ
Ad Majorem Dei Gloriam:	(*Latin*) to the greater glory of God

Francis Xavier: (1506–52) also an aristocrat, he met St Ignatius and joined with him and others in taking vows of poverty and chastity

Lorenzo Ricci: (1703–75) General of the Jesuits from 1758

the three patrons of holy youth: St Stanislaus Kostka (1550–68), St Aloysius Gonzaga (1568–91), St John Berchmans (1599–1621)

Father Peter Kenny: the founder of Clongowes Wood College

Chapter 2, Section i

Stephen is back at home in Blackrock for the summer holidays. Uncle Charles, who is himself something of an exile from the family, for he has to go into the garden outhouse to smoke his pipe, takes him shopping, and they then join Mike Flynn, who trains and times Stephen as he runs round the track in the park. On Sundays Stephen is taken on long walks out into the surrounding country by his father and grand-uncle, and the two adults talk on their favourite subjects, Irish politics and family history. Stephen is very conscious of a world of adult activity which he has not yet entered but in which he must privately prepare to do great things. In the evenings he reads *The Count of Monte Cristo* and indulges in romantic self-projections in a fantasy world.

In the real world he founds a gang with a boy, Aubrey Mills. The milkman gives the two of them rides in the milkcart out to his farm, where they are allowed to ride his horse round the field. But when autumn comes and the cows are brought in from the field to the farm-yard, the filthy cow-dung and the steaming bran-troughs turn Stephen sick.

Stephen learns that he is not to go back to Clongowes because his father is in financial difficulties. Things in home life which he has come to take for granted are changing, and each change is a shock. Stirring ambition can find no outlet. He retreats mentally to his fantasy world. The outer world of children's play seems silly by comparison.

COMMENTARY: The between-schools period is a kind of hiatus. There is a sense of not making any progress. Running round a race-track, taking walks out of Dublin and back, riding a horse around a field, and accompanying the milkman on his rounds are all circular movements that end where they begin. Mike Flynn, the running trainer with the story-book Irish name, is a flabby, decayed figure with 'lustreless' eyes who eventually has to retire to hospital. Uncle Charles drugs himself with tobacco and sits humming sentimental Irish songs, or he prays from a worn prayer-book with 'catchwords' at the bottom of each page. These fading figures are scarcely mentors for schooling the ambitious little boy, and there is no future for a winged Dedalus in going round in circles.

Since the cow is symbolic of Ireland, the day-dream Stephen indulges in of a life-time spent delivering milk to clean cottages and well-lit houses represents a temptation to easy conformity that is parallel to the later temptation to enter the priesthood and take part in distributing spiritual nourishment to his fellow-countrymen. Joyce seems to draw attention to the parallel when Stephen pictures the milkcart following the 'tramtrack' (a fixed route) on 'Rock Road' (the rock is a symbol of the Church). But the life of a farm has its sickeningly filthy side too.

The young artist takes refuge in a fantasy world inspired by literature. Restless and ambitious, he longs to find in the real world someone to match the dream-image of Mercedes, and he feels that somewhere he will meet her and in her presence lose all his weakness, fear, and immaturity.

NOTES AND GLOSSARY:

Blackrock: a coastal resort five miles from Dublin. Though Joyce was born in the Dublin suburbs, the family moved to a fashionable area in Bray when he was five. Bray was a small coastal resort thirteen miles from Dublin. The move from Bray to Blackrock' was the first downward step in the family's fortunes

The Count of Monte Cristo: by Alexandre Dumas (1802–70), French novelist. It is the story of a young sailor, Edmond Dantes, who is torn from his betrothed, Mercedes, and unjustly imprisoned for allegedly helping the exiled Napoleon in 1815. He escapes fifteen years later by taking the place of a dead fellow-prisoner, being thrown into the sea in a sack, swimming to safety, reaching Italy, and finding hidden treasure in the island cave of Monte Cristo. He is thus able to avenge himself on all who wronged him. Mercedes, though faithful in heart, was deceived into believing Dantes dead and married his enemy

Marseilles: Dantes's last interview with Mercedes is in the garden of her house in Marseilles

– Madam, I never eat muscatel grapes: Dantes replies thus to Mercedes after his return. He will not eat or drink in the house of his enemy

---

Chapter 2, Section ii

Reality breaks sharply in upon dreams. The Dedalus family has to move to Dublin, and the scene in the new house is dismal after the comfort of Blackrock.

Stephen now explores the city in detail. The quays set him dreaming of foreign places, Mercedes and Marseilles. His mother takes him to visit relations, but he remains silently angry at his own youth and the family situation. Visits recalled are one to an aunt who coos with her daughter over a newspaper photograph of a pantomime star, and one to a tenement where an old woman is chattering while he stares at a fantasy world in the glowing coals of the fire.

The third memory is of a party at Harold's Cross, a Dublin suburb. Unable to join in the other children's gaiety, Stephen is conscious of his gloomy separateness and even begins to relish his isolation. He is inwardly excited by the teasing glances of Emma Clery. After the party she accompanies him to the last tram, but he fails to take any advantage of her inviting friendliness. Instead next day he decides to write a poem to her.

Another change is in prospect. Father Conmee is arranging for Stephen and his brother Maurice to become pupils at Belvedere College without paying fees. Mr Dedalus approves of the social and academic superiority of the Jesuits and scorns the Christian Brothers' school which is the only alternative. Jauntily he tells the story he has had from Father Conmee of how Stephen protested against unjust punishment by Father Dolan, and what a great dinner-time joke it became between the two priests.

COMMENTARY: The defects in Mr Dedalus's character become more apparent. As the family fortunes decline he chatters away incoherently, venting his anger on enemies who are supposed to have done him down. Yet he is full of scorn for the Christian Brothers who work with genuine charity for the poor.

The family situation helps to turn Stephen into a lonely brooder. He proves incapable of bringing the romantic dreams of his fantasy life down to earth. On the tram after the party he reveals his weakness. He stands on the step above Emma. She keeps moving up on to his step at his side in conversation and lingering there. He senses that she is ready for him to take hold of her and kiss her. But he does nothing—just as he did nothing when Eileen put her hand in his own that day. His failure to respond fills him with gloom.

He tries to turn the experience into poetry instead. But he thinks that to write poetry he has to banish the common things from his mind—the tram, the tram-man, and the horses. As a result his verses are a quite unreal version of the experience, for the two participants stand under leafless trees in the moonlight. Having written the poem, Stephen goes to stare at his own face admiringly in the mirror. The young poet of love is more interested in himself than in Emma.

At the end of the section Stephen learns that his heroic protest against unjust punishment at Clongowes became a hilarious joke between his tormentor and his supposed protector. Joyce's technique at this point is telling. He does not describe Stephen's reaction to what must be an appalling shock. He leaves the reader, like Stephen, with the mocking laughter ringing in his ears.

NOTES AND GLOSSARY:

cheerless house: in fact the Joyces stayed little more than a year at the most at Blackrock. They moved to Dublin in late 1892 or early 1893

emerald exercise: green exercise book

A.M.D.G.: an abbreviation for *Ad Majorem Dei Gloriam* (*Latin*) 'To the greater glory of God'

second moiety notices: documents in bankruptcy proceedings

L.D.S.: an abbreviation for *Laus Deo Semper* (*Latin*) 'Praise to God always'

Belvedere: Belvedere College, run by the Jesuits and housed in the former home of the Earl of Belvedere, one of the best eighteenth-century houses in Dublin

Christian Brothers: they ran schools for poorer people, charging lower fees and giving a less academic education than the Jesuits

---

Chapter 2, Section iii

Stephen is now nearing the end of his second year at Belvedere. It is the evening of a Whitsuntide entertainment put on by the school, and Stephen has the leading role in a play. The chapel and vestry are being used as dressing-rooms. Stephen goes outside into the grounds in an inner emotional turmoil that has been with him all day. Two boys, Heron and Wallis, greet him and urge him to mimic the rector's voice and manner while acting his part in the play, that of a schoolmaster.

Heron announces that he has seen Mr Dedalus enter the theatre and ribs Stephen about the pretty girl his father has brought along to watch him. Stephen indeed is expecting Emma to come and the prospect has stirred in him the restlessness he felt at the party at Harold's Cross. Banteringly Heron flicks Stephen with his cane, calling him to 'Admit' that he has been found out. Stephen recalls a parallel demand made during his first term at Belvedere. Mr Tate, the English master, publicly charged him with heresy in his weekly essay. Stephen retracted the offending statement, but a few days later he was baited in the road by Heron and two other boys. He insisted that Byron was the greatest poet and ridiculed Heron's preference for Tennyson. Whereupon they seized him and Heron slashed at him with a cane, requiring him to 'Admit' that Byron was no good.

The memory no longer causes resentment, and Stephen is preoccupied with the thought of Emma sitting in the audience waiting for his appearance. He is called in to get dressed. He dislikes his part and finds some of the lines vulgar, but the thought of Emma's eyes watching him gives him confidence, and when he comes on stage the play generates its own vitality and carries him on its tide. Afterwards he dashes out in feverish anticipation only to discover that there is no sign of Emma with his family. Crushed in spirit, he makes an excuse and rushes off, not caring where, till he finds himself in a dismal, stinking corner of the city.

COMMENTARY: Stephen is no shrinking weakling at Belvedere. He has been given the main part in the school play. He is recognised along with Heron as a leader. Yet any casual reference to his father by a schoolfellow fills him with fearful apprehension. The family situation is an embarrassment. The brush with Mr Tate over the essay came at a time when the family's descent into near-poverty was still souring him. That was why in his leisure time he turned to writers whose rebellious, satirical attitudes influenced him.

The repeated demand that he should 'Admit' his error plays its part in the continuing theme which began with the call to him as an infant to 'apologise' and will reach a climax with the retreat priest's call to repentance. Stephen boldly claims supreme greatness for a poet, Byron, who was execrated by respectable society for his immorality, who was driven to exile by social ostracism, and who gave vent to the volcanic turbulence of the lawless romantic spirit. Yet when Heron is angry at the peremptory order issued to them as older boys, Stephen feels no urge to break his own habit of obedience. Instead he is becoming insulated in his mind, preoccupied with his own dreams, and deaf to the numerous voices that urge him to do this or that—to be a gentleman, or a good Catholic, or a firm nationalist, or a defender of Irish culture. They all sound hollow.

Ironically enough, in the artificial world of drama he finds himself involved in the boyish excitement of those around him and capable of achieving an assured performance in a fictional role. His success in the stage world of illusion is the result of another illusion—that Emma is watching him and will be there to meet him afterwards. Once more the reality is a bitter let-down after the fervent anticipation.

NOTES AND GLOSSARY:

tabernacle: an ornamented receptacle for holding the bread which has been consecrated at Mass and which is therefore called 'the Blessed Sacrament'

the play: Joyce took part in such a play at Belvedere. It was a dramatic version of F. Anstey's (1856–1934) novel, *Vice Versa* (1882). Acting the part of the schoolmaster, he mimicked the rector, Father Henry

after beads:	after the daily recitation of the Rosary
one sure five:	a sure thing (expression used in the game of bil-
	liards)
Confiteor:	(*Latin*) 'I confess'; opening of the confession
Captain Marryat:	(1792–1848) a writer of old-fashioned, straight-
	forward sea-stories once popular with boys
Newman:	Cardinal Newman (1801–1900), the great Catholic
	thinker whose prose style is so fine that Stephen
	can honestly praise it without reference to what it
	says. Newman was the founder of the Catholic
	University in Dublin which became University Col-
	lege
Lord Tennyson:	(1809–92) poet laureate and the most celebrated
	poet of Victorian England. While Byron was a
	rebellious figure who shocked society, Tennyson
	was a pillar of respectability

Chapter 2, Section iv

Stephen goes with his father by night train to Cork. Mr Dedalus drinks whisky and talks sentimentally about his youthful days in Cork. He is going to witness the final auction of his heavily mortgaged property. From the train the two of them go to a hotel bedroom. Mr Dedalus sings cheerfully as he shaves in the morning, and at breakfast he questions the waiter about local people and places. Stephen realises that the waiter is thinking of the present, his father of the past.

Mr Dedalus and Stephen walk to Queen's College where a talkative porter conducts Mr Dedalus on a sentimental tour of his old haunts. In the anatomy theatre Mr Dedalus searches for the desk on which he carved his initials, and Stephen is shocked to find the word *Foetus* repeatedly carved. Mr Dedalus goes on recalling former companions and experiences as they leave the college, while Stephen feels sick at heart. His father's clichés urge him to 'mix with gentlemen' and they sentimentalise the past, but Stephen feels inwardly isolated from reality by failure to find in the outer world anything that matches the wild demands of his own heart.

After the sale of the property Stephen follows his father who makes a tour of the bars, playing the old Corkman. Stephen feels humiliated by his father's performance. Market sellers, barmaids, and old friends play up to Mr Dedalus's sentimental bonhomie. They tell Stephen he is like his father, pretend he has traces of a Cork accent, ask him his views of the Cork girls, and assure him that his father was a great ladies' man. Hollow words of admiration go to Mr Dedalus's head. Ordering more drinks, he boasts of his voice and his vigour. The episode ends in mutual self-congratulation by the drinkers. Stephen feels older than they are.

COMMENTARY: The Cork visit serves to detach Stephen irrevocably from his father. Tagging on behind him, he sees the hollowness of his garrulous bonhomie, is shamed by the way he can be duped by an obsequious college servant, is embarrassed by his flirtatiousness with barmaids, and disgusted by his excessive drinking. The shame reinforces the humiliation already felt in his ambiguous position at Belvedere as a leader whose taste of authority is spoiled by the sordidness of his home background and his private thoughts.

The shock caused by the word *Foetus* is sharp because he has assumed that his personal obsession with anatomical and sexual images was a crude private malady, and here he finds a trace of the same monstrous evil in the outer world. But, as for the outer world of shops and sunshine, he feels so isolated from it that he tries to strengthen his grip on reality by reciting his name and defining where he is. Even the memory of childhood seems to slip away from him. The little boy that was fades into nothingness.

By the end of the episode Stephen is sadly aware that he has never himself tasted the kind of youthful pleasure and companionship on which his father and his cronies look back so nostalgically. The only movement within him is that of lust. He quotes to himself Shelley's lines on the moon: they fit his sense of life's melancholy meaninglessness.

NOTES AND GLOSSARY:

come-all-yous:	songs of a jolly, boisterous kind of which a typical verse or chorus would begin, 'Come all you good people . . . '
drisheens:	puddings made of sheep's intestines and meal
the Groceries:	most grocers sold alcoholic drink as well as foodstuffs
maneens:	(*dialect*) little chaps
slim jim:	marshmallow powdered with coconut
Dilectus:	a book of selected Latin quotations
Tempora mutantur et nos mutamur in illis:	(*Latin*) 'Times change and we change with them'

Chapter 2, Section v

Stephen has won an exhibition and essay prize of thirty-three pounds. He and his father go to cash the prize cheque at the Bank of Ireland. The bank building was once the Irish House of Commons, and Mr Dedalus recalls great parliamentarians of the days before the Union.

Stephen treats the family to a spending spree on food, theatres, and presents. He plans a reorganisation of the household and sets himself up as banker. When the money is spent, the ordinary routine is restored.

The return to poverty revives sexual longings. Stephen's private reveries idealise an innocent girl by day and turn her into a creature of lust at night. He takes up again the habit of wandering the Dublin streets in the autumn evenings. Sometimes he is haunted by idealised romantic figures from literature, but such fantasies give way to crude, unassuaged lust. Thus one night he wanders into the brothel area. Women move in vivid dresses from house to house and he is intoxicated by their perfume, by the yellow gas lamps, open doors and lighted halls. A prostitute accosts him, and the scene shifts to her bedroom where she initiates him into the sexual act.

COMMENTARY: The prize money enables Stephen to make a grand attempt to establish order and good taste at home in the face of the flood of sordidness overwhelming the family. It proves futile. So does his attempt to improve his own personal relations with the family by spending money. At the end of his experiment he is as isolated as ever by inner shame and ill-feeling.

Stephen's sexual hunger involves both the romantic aspirations of a sensitive poetic mind and the physical urges of adolescence. His disquiet is increased by the guilt of consciously wanting to sin and to involve another person in sin. His habit of self-dramatisation inflates his natural sexual hunger into the lust of a prowling animal. The prostitute gives him two things he desperately needs in appeasing his sexual hunger and making him feel sure of himself.

NOTES AND GLOSSARY:

Hely Hutchinson: John Hely Hutchinson (1724–94), Henry Flood (1732–91), and Henry Grattan (1746–1820) were distinguished eighteenth-century Irish parliamentarians; Charles Kendal Bushe (1767–1843) was a judge and a renowned orator

Ingomar: a highly sentimental adaptation made in 1851 by Maria Anne Lovell of a German play by Friederich Halm (1806–71). The wild-spirited Ingomar is tamed by love for a Greek maiden

The Lady of Lyons: a play by Bulwer-Lytton (1803–73), first produced in 1838. It is a drama of absurdly romantic extravagance. Its hero, Claude Melnotte, with whom Stephen later identifies himself, is a young poet from a poor home who aspires to the hand of a beautiful rich young woman and reveals astonishing nobility of character

Chapter 3, Section i

Stephen is at school at a mathematics lesson, hungrily looking forward to his evening meal. He pictures what will happen afterwards, as he makes his roundabout way to the brothel area. Apparently this has become his regular practice, and he now feels icily indifferent about it. On his first coition he expected to find himself inwardly wounded, instead of which he felt a new peace between body and soul. What brought back inner turmoil was the knowledge that he was committing mortal sin and seeking damnation. Yet he still plays his privileged part in chapel as prefect of the sodality of the Virgin Mary. Indeed he finds solace in the rich imagery in which the praise of Mary is recited.

The lesson ends. Boys chatter. One suggests that Stephen should play his game of asking theological questions of the rector when he comes in for the catechism instruction. Stephen still enjoys pursuing theological niceties even though he is lost in sin. But when the rector arrives he does not turn to the catechism but announces a retreat in honour of St Francis Xavier. He then reminds the boys of St Francis's faith and zeal in winning souls for God. And he stresses Francis's continuing power in heaven to pray for people in grief or for sinners in grave need of repentance. The last point and the penetrating gaze with which the rector fixes his pupils causes Stephen's heart to wither within him.

COMMENTARY: As Stephen sits at his desk the mathematical equation he is working on widens out down the page, then narrows again towards the conclusion. The theme of opening and closing was touched on when Stephen played with his ears in the refectory (1, ii). The image of opening and closing, as in the birth and quenching of stars, seems to match the experience of his soul which moves outwards from sin to sin, shedding its burning stars, then folding itself back into darkness and coldness. This highly fanciful projection of his sexual life in cosmic terms illustrates Stephen's capacity for egotistic exaggeration, as does his projection of himself as a lost soul. Moreover, the way he despises his schoolfellows and affects disgust at the 'dull piety' of ordinary folk reveals a distasteful snobbishness. There is posturing in the way he dramatises his own urge to penitence in terms of romantic chivalry and with sensuous relish of the Virgin Mary's femininity. Yet a voice of genuinely critical self-examination is heard through Stephen's exaggerations. He can see proof of St James's claim that one offence involves all other offences in the way his lust has bred pride, contempt, covetousness, envy, and the other deadly sins.

NOTES AND GLOSSARY:

sanctifying grace: (or 'habitual' grace) the divine impulse to do good normally conveyed through the sacraments

actual grace: a divine impulse to do good which may come even to the unbaptised

sodality: a religious guild formed for some special purpose, in this case for devotion to the Virgin Mary

the little office: a weekly service incorporating recitation of biblical passages and prayers

psalms of prophecy: *Old Testament* psalms interpreted symbolically in *New Testament* terms

her royal lineage: as descended from King David

Quasi cedrus exaltata in Libanon . . . : (*Latin*) 'I was lifted up like the Cedar in Lebanon and like the cypress on Mount Sion. I was lifted up like the palm tree in Gades and like the rose-bushes in Jericho. I was lifted up like the beautiful olive on the plains and like the plane-tree by the river in the glades. I gave off fragrant perfume like cinnamon and balsam, and sweet scent like choice myrrh.'
The passage is from one of the apocryphal books of the Bible, Ecclesiasticus 24: 13–15 and is used in the 'little office'

bright and musical, telling of heaven and infusing peace: quotation from 'The Glories of Mary', in *Discourses to Mixed Congregations* (1849), by Cardinal Newman

game ball: a piece of luck

catechism: an instruction book of Christian doctrine

sentence of saint James: from the Bible, James 2: 10 – 'For whosoever shall keep the whole law, and yet offend in one point, he is guilty of all.'

Chapter 3, Section ii

The retreat has begun. Stephen is sitting in chapel listening to the first address given by the retreat conductor, Father Arnall. He praises St Francis Xavier, then dwells briefly on the purpose of a retreat as a temporary withdrawal from day-to-day life for concentration on spiritual matters. The subjects of his retreat addresses are to be the Four Last Things: death, judgement, hell, and heaven. The boys are urged to put from their minds for a time all considerations other than the fact that they have been sent into the world for one purpose only – to do God's will and to save their souls. The sermon sends Stephen home in deep despondency. He feels disgusted with his filthy wickedness and reduced to a state of spiritless despair.

Next day's sermons on death and judgement transform spiritlessness into fear. Father Arnall conjures up a picture of death, burial, and judgement. The individual soul will appear before God at the Judgement to be directed to heaven, purgatory, or hell. That is the 'particular judgement' that every individual faces. There is also the 'general judgement' which the whole human race will face on the world's last day, when Christ will return to earth to call the just to his side and to banish the unjust to hell. So everyone must die and be judged. One must be prepared for it at any moment. Death is fearsome to the sinner, but not to the righteous.

Stephen feels that every word is meant for him. The image of judgement shatters all peace of mind until he manages to conjure up a romantic picture of repentance at Emma's side.

Father Arnall begins his sermon on hell by recalling that Adam and Eve were created by God in order that the human race might take up the places in heaven left vacant by the Fall of the Angels. Lucifer, the angel of light, fell into disobedience through the sin of pride. *Non serviam*, 'I will not serve', that decision was the basis of his rebellion, and he and his followers were cast into hell for ever. Thus Father Arnall recounts the story of the temptation and fall of Adam and Eve, and their banishment from Eden into a world of toil and grief. When God in his mercy sent his only Son to redeem the world, men's response to this gesture was to crucify their Saviour like a criminal.

Father Arnall then launches into a lengthy description, bloodcurdling and horrific in its detail, of the pains of hell which the damned will suffer. He ends his sermon with the hope that none of those present may ever have to endure these horrors, but Stephen comes out of chapel trembling and shaking. An announcement that confessions are now being heard in chapel brings a chill to his heart. He must find some other place to uncover his shame.

Back in chapel Father Arnall renews his theme. This morning he spoke of the physical torments of hell. This evening he will consider its spiritual torments. He analyses these under five heads: (1) pain of loss, the torment of separation from God; (2) pain of conscience with its threefold sting—(a) embitterment of remembering past pleasures, (b) remorse at seeing the full hideousness of sin, (c) realisation of how a life-time's opportunities for repentance have been wilfully thrown away; (3) pain of extension—hell allows earth's separate torments to be endured all at once; (4) pain of intensity, the lack of any relief to moderate this suffering, and the impossibility of becoming inured by habit to tortures that are infinitely varied and fierce; (5) the eternity of pain.

Father Arnall dwells insistently on the unbroken finality of always knowing misery and never knowing relief. Such is the justice of God for those who die in mortal sin, and if people feel surprise that a single sin can provoke such punishment, that is because they fail to comprehend the hideousness of sin. A single momentary sin brought down Lucifer and drove Adam and Eve from Eden. Since the Son of God came to earth to suffer and die in order to save mankind, every sin we commit is a renewal of the mockery and the wounding of Christ. Father Arnall concludes by hoping that what he has said may strengthen those in a state of grace and may help to restore to a state of grace any who have strayed. He asks the boys to join him in prayer for repentance, reminding them of God's mercy and love. Stephen cannot move his tongue, but he prays with his heart.

COMMENTARY: The retreat sermons have a magnificent rhetorical force and often a powerful emotive appeal. They begin on a calm and reasonable note in evident sincerity, yet before long, both in substance and in tone, they lapse into burlesque. Imagery of heaped-up bodies confined within walls four thousand miles thick, of brains boiling in skulls and entrails turning to red-hot pulp is plainly absurd. The contrast between the ingenuity of God's tortures and the mercy and love attributed to him is too glaring to be missed. Moreover, Father Arnall seems to be obsessed. When the time comes for the fourth sermon, which ought to be about the last of the Four Last Things, namely heaven, he forgets the subject and turns to a second orgy of rhetoric on the pains of hell.

Stephen's response contains its excesses too. Father Arnall's associations with Clongowes set him picturing himself as a child again, and the sermons are indeed to thrust the young artist back into a state of childish submission. In the first shock of guilt, shame is redoubled by the thought of Emma. Now that God and the Virgin Mary are inaccessibly remote from his filthiness, it is only by picturing Emma at his side that he can rise from his abject inertia. The day-dream of himself, hand in hand with Emma, being forgiven and comforted by a sympathetic Virgin Mary, is a comic piece of self-projection. So too, when overcoats and raincoats along the corridor walls begin to look to him like decapitated corpses hanging from gibbets and his brain begins to simmer and bubble, the element of humour is unmistakable.

NOTES AND GLOSSARY:
— *Remember only thy last things and thou shalt not sin for ever*: the text is *not* from the Old Testament book Ecclesiastes but from the apocryphal book Ecclesiasticus (7: 36)
The stars of heaven were falling . . . : the imagery here is taken from the Book of Revelation, chapters 6 and 10
Valley of Jehoshaphat: traditionally regarded as the scene of the Lord's coming to bring judgment on the world— on the basis of two sentences in Joel 3: 2 and 12

And lo the supreme judge is coming!: the description of Christ's Second Coming derives from Matthew 25: 31ff.

***Depart from me, ye cursed* . . . :** Matthew 25: 41

O you hypocrites, O, you whited sepulchres: Matthew 23: 27

Addison: Joseph Addison (1672–1719) was reported to have said on his death-bed: 'See in what peace a Christian can die.'

O grave, where is thy victory?: St Paul's sentences from I Corinthians 15: 55 (sentences reversed)

It is not like earthly beauty . . . bright and musical: quotation from Cardinal Newman's 'The Glories of Mary' in *Discourses to Mixed Congregations* (1849)

Forty days and forty nights the rain would fall: as when God punished mankind by the Flood. See the Bible, Genesis 7: 4

In the plain of Damascus: this seems to be Father Arnall's own location of the Garden of Eden

saint Anselm: (*c.*1033–1109) mediaeval theologian, Archbishop of Canterbury

the Babylonian furnace: into which Nebuchadnezzar cast Shadrach, Meshach, and Abednego (see the Bible, Daniel 3: 13ff). Its heat was miraculously quenched

saint Bonaventure: (1221–74) Italian-born scholar who became Minister General of the Franciscan Order

Saint Catherine of Siena: (1347–80) a nun who dedicated herself to contemplation and to service of the needy, and whose piety won many followers

book of spiritual exercises: St Ignatius Loyola wrote a series of meditations and rules for overcoming the passions and giving the soul to God

Saint Thomas: St Thomas Aquinas (*c.*1225–74), called the 'angelic doctor', was the greatest philosopher and theologian of the medieval Church

Pope Innocent the Third: (1160–1216), Pope from 1198

mortal sin: sin wilfully committed with clear awareness of guilt which deprives the soul of sanctifying grace, as opposed to 'venial sin', sin of lesser gravity which does not so deprive the soul

---

Chapter 3, Section iii

After dinner Stephen goes up to his room in inner ferment, feeling that death may strike at any moment. He is surrounded by faces, eyes, presences, and murmuring voices, but manages to pray simply for forgiveness before getting into bed. Horror of his filthy sins produces a nightmare that sends him to the window gasping for fresh air. In tears he prays to the Virgin Mary for guidance.

At nightfall he leaves the house to go to confession. Walking the dark streets, he longs to be free and sinless, and imagines that dirty girls at the roadside may be radiant in God's eyes and dearer to God than he. He asks an old woman if there is a chapel nearby and she directs him there.

Inside the chapel he kneels among those waiting near the confessional and prays for humility to match that of the simple souls around him. A priest enters the confessional box and, one by one, the other penitents go up and murmur their confessions. Stephen realises that there is still time to change his mind, but he is firm with himself, duly takes his place in the confessional, and recounts his sins. The priest is gentle, but implores him to give up his sin and to pray for help to do so. With tears in his eyes Stephen hears the words of absolution, then returns to his place in the nave to say the penance the priest has laid on him.

He is now filled with joy by the knowledge of forgiveness. He lives in a waking dream through to next morning, when he attends the Mass at the end of the retreat. As he receives the sacrament he is ecstatic with happiness.

COMMENTARY: Though Stephen is genuinely horrified by his wickedness and terrified of its consequences, the imagery of remorse and penitence is so exaggerated that he seems more like an imaginative artist projecting a larger-than-life picture of himself than the simple-hearted penitent he aspires to be. The nightmare scene of rankness, stench, and dung, and the hideous semi-bestialised creatures who inhabit it, are grotesque. Even Stephen's attempts at simple-heartedness have a self-conscious, posturing air.

The happiness produced by absolution has too its over-posturing, egotistic side. The joy of possessing a soul once more 'made fair and holy' has a precious, self-conscious air, and the mental transformation of the living room at home is a little too good to be true.

NOTES AND GLOSSARY:

He once had meant to come to earth . . . : quoted from Cardinal Newman's 'The Glories of Mary'

capuchin: an off-shoot of the Franciscan order: the brown habit includes a pointed cowl ('capuche') like that of St Francis

ciborium: a chalice-shaped vessel with a lid, used to hold the sacramental bread of the Mass

− *Corpus Domini nostri*: (*Latin*) 'The Body of our Lord', the formula used when offering the sacramental bread to the communicants

— In vitam eternam: (*Latin*) 'to everlasting life': the full formula is 'the Body of our Lord Jesus Christ which was given for you preserve your body and soul to everlasting life'

Chapter 4, Section i

Stephen now subjects himself to a rigorous personal discipline of private prayer and daily attendance at Mass. he carries rosary beads in his pocket and daily offers up three rounds of prayer for strengthening in faith, hope, and charity. On successive days of the week he prays for the seven gifts of the Holy Spirit to counter the defilement of the seven deadly sins. He also subjects himself to regular mortifications that discipline each of his senses methodically. He is still worried by failure to establish emotional relationships with others, but he visits the church to pray before the Blessed Sacrament reserved on the altar. Though sometimes he questions the motives of his repentance, he takes comfort in the subsequent improvement of his life as sure proof of true contrition.

COMMENTARY: Stephen's spiritual and moral reformation is described with ironic humour, at its sharpest when his sense of the effectiveness of his prayer in the world above is likened to the operation of a cash-register which sends figures shooting up. Again his state of intellectual submission is so extreme that rational judgement is bypassed and he finds the traditional imagery of the relationship of the three Persons of the Trinity (Father, Son, and Holy Ghost) all the more acceptable by reason of its lofty incomprehensibility. Joyce shows Stephen drifting further and further away from reality. Human passions are replaced by a vague sense of divine love and power diffused through the world with such fullness that he himself feels redundant. When he meditates on love it is not real people or real action that come to his mind but celebrated pictures of people praying. The irony here is sharp. Stephen's life of prayer is so contrived that the pulse of life is lost in recourse to aesthetic symbols.

Some of Stephen's devices for mortifying the various senses are comic—such as submitting himself to the most unpleasant smells he can find, or not properly drying his face and neck after washing. The whole programme of self-discipline smacks of subordinating the real to the ideal, as does the fact that 'spiritual communions' made on private visits to the Blessed Sacrament seem more moving than his actual receipt of the sacrament in the Mass. Unctuous linguistic echoes from books of instruction, exhortation, and devotion give his reformed way of life a second-hand flavour comparable to that of his earlier indulgence in Byronic romanticism. Stephen's ultimate attitude in this section is a mood of self-satisfaction with his amended life. He is still looking at himself admiringly in a mirror.

NOTES AND GLOSSARY:

sovereign pontiff: the Pope
centuries of days: periods of a hundred days
quarantines: periods of forty days (the suffering of souls in purgatory may be lightened by prayers for them)
suffrage: prayers for the souls of the departed
canonical: according to canon law
works of supererogation: acts not enjoined by duty or obligation but going beyond merely keeping the rule
rosary: string of beads used to assist the memory in moving through fifteen subjects of meditation (also called the 'Rosary')
chaplets: each chaplet comprises five decades: each decade is associated with one 'mystery' and contains ten recitations of the 'Hail Mary', one 'Our Father', and a 'Gloria Patri'
joyful mysteries: the Annunciation, the Visitation, the Nativity of Christ, the Presentation of Christ in the Temple, the finding of the child Jesus in the Temple
sorrowful mysteries: the Agony in Gethsemane, the Scourging of Jesus, His crowning with thorns, His carrying of the cross, His crucifixion
glorious mysteries: the Resurrection, the Ascension, the Descent of the Holy Spirit at Pentecost, the Assumption of the Virgin Mary, the Coronation of the Virgin Mary
seven gifts of the Holy Ghost: wisdom, understanding, counsel, fortitude, knowledge, piety, fear of the Lord
seven deadly sins: pride, covetousness, lust, envy, gluttony, anger, sloth
Paraclete: the Holy Spirit
saint Alphonsus Liguori: (1696−1787) Italian saint, founder of the Redemptorist order. He was known for preaching simply to the heart. His many devotional writings include *Visits to the Blessed Sacrament*: it interweaves with the prayers some quotations from the Song of Solomon which can be allegorically interpreted
Bidding her arise as for espousal and come away: see the Bible, Song of Solomon 2: 13—'Arise, my love, my fair one, and come away'
Inter ubera mea commorabitur: (*Latin*) 'He will lie between my breasts', Song of Solomon 1: 13

Chapter 4, Section ii

Stephen has been summoned for an interview with the director of studies, who begins conversation with small-talk. Coming to the point, he asks Stephen whether he has ever felt a vocation to the priesthood. The priesthood is the greatest honour that God can bestow; its authority surpasses all earthly authority. Stephen is sensitive to the director's invitation as an offer of secret knowledge and power but, taking leave of him at the door, he sees four young men striding past, arms linked, singing to a concertina. The contrast between this scene and the 'mirthless mask' of the priest's face stirs disquiet within him, an instinct of repugnance against the cold orderliness of Jesuit life, and its implicit threat to his freedom.

He crosses the bridge over the Tolka to make his way home. He smiles to think of the disorders and oddities of the life he has opted for. At home remains of tea litter the table. His brothers and sisters tell him that there is another removal afoot, the landlord being about to put them out.

COMMENTARY: The lure of priestly power has long tempted Stephen. He has pictured himself performing priestly functions. The romanticised picture of the priestly role at the altar or in the confessional can still appeal to him, but his pride in his own isolation is stronger. His destiny is to learn for himself, not cut off from the world, but subject to the world's snares. When he gets home he brings the same imaginative sensitivity to bear on the family scene as he brought to bear on the office of priesthood. His brothers and sisters, as is their wont, break into song to escape the sordid reality of their home, and he detects overtones of weariness and pain in their innocent young voices like the melancholy note in the verse of Virgil.

NOTES AND GLOSSARY:

The capuchin dress: the capuchins clung to their cassocks all the time, while other orders exchanged them for suits when going out of the cloister

− Les jupes: (*French*) skirts

a muff: an untutored novice

Lord Macaulay: (1800−59) English historian and essayist

Victor Hugo: (1802−85) eminent French writer

Louis Veuillot: (1813−83) French journalist, a virulent and bigotted Catholic moralist who condemned writers on moralistic grounds

power of the keys: authority to forgive sins and thereby open the gate of heaven (see the Bible, Matthew 16: 18−19)

thurible: the censer which holds the incense

chasuble:	the vestment worn by a priest in celebrating Mass
tunicle:	the outer liturgical garment of the sub-deacon
high mass:	Mass with full ceremonial at which a deacon and a sub-deacon assist the celebrant
humeral veil:	a silk shawl laid round the shoulders and covering the hands: the sub-deacon holds the paten with it during the Mass
paten:	the dish (usually gold or silver) in which the bread is placed at the celebration of Mass
dalmatic:	a garment worn by deacons at high Mass: it is ornamented by two stripes running over the shoulders from front to back
Ite, missa est:	(*Latin*) 'Go, you are dismissed', formula used at the end of Mass
acolyte:	a server
Simon Magus:	the sorcerer who practised in Samaria and whom St Peter rebuked for trying to buy spiritual power from the Apostles with money

eat and drink damnation to himself, not discerning the Lord's body:
Stephen is quoting St Paul's warning—'For he that eateth and drinket unworthily, eateth and drinketh damnation to himself, not discerning the Lord's body' (see the Bible, I Corinthians 11: 29)

Melchisedec:	Old Testament figure representative of the kind of priesthood later attributed to Christ
novena:	nine days' private or public devotion to obtain some special grace

giving utterance, like the voice of nature herself... : the quotation is from Cardinal Newman's *An Essay in Aid of a Grammar of Assent* (1881)

Chapter 4, Section iii

Stephen is waiting for his father who is making enquiries for him about a place at the university. The prospect of going to the university is like breaking through forces that have tried to keep him in subjection. Turning towards the sea to cross the wooden bridge to the island called 'the Bull', he meets a group of Christian Brothers coming the other way, the bridge trembling under their tread. He is aware of their simple humility, their piety, and their good works, but as he leaves the trembling bridge for firm land, he knows that it is in the magic of words that he himself finds harmony between the outer scene and the inner emotional life.

The voices of students bathing nearby are heard, mocking his name, and he senses the destiny prophetically represented by 'Dedalus', for Daedalus was the great artificer who tried to fly above the sea. He takes off shoes and stockings and climbs down on to the sand. He sees a girl standing in midstream staring out to sea, her legs and thighs bared. She has a wonderful girlish beauty and she looks at him long and lingeringly. She is a perfect image of the call to life that he is now answering.

COMMENTARY: In pacing between Byron's public house and Clontarf chapel, Stephen is moving between places representative respectively of the literary life and the Church. His mother's opposition to the idea of his going to the university is in line with her regret at his fading faith, and Stephen is aware of the process of becoming severed from her. Turning towards the sea and crossing the bridge have clear symbolic overtones, and as Stephen looks back to land the city wears a tired air of age and long subjection. These are the things he is to escape from like the clouds sailing westward above him.

What follows next is the climax of the book. In thinking about Daedalus, Stephen's spirit soars above the world. This is a kind of 'resurrection' for him. It frees him from the hopelessness and lifelessness of ecclesiastical duty. He is shaking off the grave clothes of fear and shame, and rising to a life of freedom and power in the calling of the creative artist. At the sight of the wading girl Stephen exclaims, 'Heavenly God!' and the outburst marks a new 'conversion'. As following his conversion after the retreat he moved haltingly and tremblingly into the 'cave' of his bedroom, so now after this new conversion, flushed and trembling, he strides out across the open sands to 'greet the advent' of his new life. The girl's image has concentrated in one revelation the call to life and creativity. As in his bedroom he dreamed of natural desolation, excrement, and hideous bestial creatures, so now he dreams of a new world waking to life in the dawn like an unfolding flower.

NOTES AND GLOSSARY:
— *Whose feet are as the feet of harts and underneath the everlasting arms*: the quotation is from Cardinal Newman's *The Idea of a University* (1852)
Thingmote: the Danish governing council
a stuff in the kisser: (*slang*) a blow in the face
Stephanos: (*Greek*) garland
Bous: (*Greek*) ox

Chapter 5, Section i

Stephen is having breakfast in the now squalid home, fiddling with tickets for the clothes the family has pawned under false names. He is late for his lectures and when his father calls out angrily from upstairs he is hurried out by the back door. His morning walk through Dublin now carries, stage by stage, fanciful literary associations evoked by his surroundings. A clock striking eleven reminds him of the lectures he is missing and he pictures fellow students at work. Cranly comes to mind. His pale, priestlike face fascinates Stephen, who has unburdened himself volubly to him. Cranly always listens in silence. He has a deadpan literalness that can empty words of meaning, while Stephen finds inspiration in the richness of words

Stephen thinks too of Davin, a student with the mental bluntness and heaviness of a peasant, who is a fierce nationalist. Once Davin told him how a peasant woman, late at night, invited him to share her bed, but he went on his way. And Stephen goes on his way when a flower-girl stops him to try to sell him some flowers. Reaching the college, he finds the dean of studies trying to light the fire in the physics theatre, and the dean engages him in conversation about his studies.

The professor enters and gives his lecture amid whispered backchat among the students. Afterwards, in the entrance hall, MacCann, a political progressivist and a teetotaller, is collecting signatures in support of the Czar's appeal for international peace. Cranly has signed. When MacCann attempts to get Stephen to sign a ring of students gathers round, expecting an altercation. MacCann appeals idealistically for the cause of disarmament and progress. He calls Stephen a reactionary for his assumed superiority to practical matters, and in reply Stephen mocks the photograph of the Czar as an icon, a bogus Jesus, then goes off with Cranly and Temple. They make for the ball-alley and find Davin there. Temple tries to involve Stephen in intellectual conversation while Cranly repels him. Stephen mocks Davin for signing a petition that seems incongruous with his rebellious nationalism. Davin wishes Stephen would join the nationalist cause, but Stephen dropped out of the Irish class partly, it seems, in anger because he saw Father Moran, the instructor, flirting with Emma. He cannot allow his life to be mortgaged to the past or support a cause whose great leaders have invariably been betrayed. He sees the inheritance of nationality, language, and religion as nets preventing his soul from flight.

Stephen now goes off with Lynch, a tough, muscular fellow. To this unlikely character he propounds his aesthetic theory with great solemnity. Lynch interrupts with crude repartees. Stephen persists, pausing only for the passage nearby of a noisy dray laden with old iron and for the intervention of Donovan who brings news of examination results.

Stephen's aesthetic theory: Stephen defines pity and terror. Pity unites the mind of the observer with the sufferer; terror unites it with the cause of the suffering. Accidental calamity is not truly tragic. Tragic emotion is properly static. It is improper art which excites kinetic feelings of desire or loathing, as pornography and didacticism do. Art is the attempt to embody an image of beauty in sound or shape or colour. It is man's way of arranging what appeals to the senses or to the mind for an aesthetic purpose. The beautiful is what can be pleasurably apprehended by the senses or the mind. Static reception of this pleasure precludes the moral element which, instead of satisfying, stirs feelings of desire or loathing. Truth satisfies the intellect, while beauty satisfies the imagination.

How does the imagination work in this respect? Different races admire different types of female beauty. Apparently, therefore, beauty involves 'relations of the sensible' which are detected by one person through one form and by another person through another form. Aquinas said, 'Three things are needed for beauty; wholeness, harmony, and radiance'. The wholeness of a thing is what sets it apart from everything else as a single entity. The harmony is the unity of its various parts in the whole. The radiance of the thing is the quality that makes it itself and nothing else. The three phases of artistic appreciation correspond to these three constituents of the beautiful. The mind is seized by its wholeness, fascinated by its harmony, and enchanted by its radiance.

Art can be divided into three forms—the lyrical, the epical, and the dramatic. The lyrical form is the direct expression of emotion. In the epical form the artist projects the centre of emotional gravity outside himself so that his personality passes into the narration itself. In the dramatic form vitality belongs to the characters themselves and the artist's statement is totally impersonalised. The artist, like God himself, becomes transcendently detached from his creation.

At the end of the section Emma is seen under the library arcade, and Stephen broods about her attitude, first harshly, then indulgently.

COMMENTARY: In many respects Stephen, now a dedicated artist, seems no more human than Stephen the devout reformed Catholic. This section shows him at loggerheads with his fellow-creatures. If there was romantic exaggeration in the way he felt at one with them after his repentance, there is now a sharp severance from them in feeling and attitude. His father's and mother's reproaches (not unjust towards a student from a poor home who cannot get up in time for his lectures) are put mentally on the same level as the screeching of a maniac nun. In his walk through Dublin he congratulates himself on being in the midst of common lives when in fact he is quite out of touch. The real Dublin and its people are just a backcloth for literary reverie and speculation.

Having abandoned the Church, Stephen makes a priestlike confessor of Cranly, who will conveniently listen and not answer back. He seems to choose as friends and confidants students who are mere sounding-boards for his own rhetoric. He is patronising towards Davin's unquestioning peasant acceptance of Catholicism and extreme nationalism. Yet Davin's night experience in the hills suggests that the archetypal countrywoman of Ireland will give herself to the patriotic nationalist with a responsiveness that the artist Stephen never elicits. When the dean of studies tries to show a proper interest in his work, Stephen focuses mentally on the man's limitations, and wastes a good deal of rhetoric in decrying them and in fancifully elaborating them—this in spite of the fact that he is compelled to concede that the dean is a rather decent sort.

Stephen adopts a superior, indeed supercilious air in controversy. MacCann's earnest eagerness for practical causes produces a community effort in the form of a petition from which Stephen can only isolate himself in aloof detachment. Going about putting everybody else right and puncturing their various ideas with clever epigrammatic tartness is not the way to win friends. The other students are for the most part surprisingly tolerant. The pedantic way in which Stephen presents his aesthetic theory, disregarding the cheerful banter of Lynch, is the mark of a humourless prig. In the structure of the book as a whole the theory is the only statement to compare in substantiality and logic with Father Arnall's sermons. The rhetoric of the rebellious artist's creed turns out to be as extravagantly remote from living reality as the rhetoric of Father Arnall's, for as the theorising on beauty ends, the living beauty, Emma, is glimpsed and Stephen's immediate response is one of bitterness and mistrust. Then there blows a breath of fresh air as he asks himself whether he may have misjudged her. Briefly the reader wonders whether he may after all begin to make contact, but the highly poetic image of her as a bird is not promising.

NOTES AND GLOSSARY:

Gerhart Hauptmann: (1863–1946) German dramatist, novelist, and poet who wrote both naturalistic drama and romantic fantasies

sloblands: muddy ground

Guido Cavalcanti: (1259?–1300) Florentine poet, friend of Dante

Ben Jonson: (1572–1637) after Shakespeare the major Elizabethan dramatist and poet

waistcoateers: (*archaic*) common prostitutes

Aristotle: the ancient Greek philosopher (384–322BC) to whom Aquinas was indebted

Synopsis Philosophiae Scholasticae ad mentem divi Thomae: (*Latin*) 'Summary of Scholastic Philosophy according to the thought of Saint Thomas'

ivoire, avorio, ebur: (*French, Italian, Latin*) ivory

India mittit ebur: (*Latin*) 'India exports ivory'

Contrahit orator, variant in carmine vates: (*Latin*) 'The speaker sums
    things up but poets elaborate them in verse'
in tanto discrimine: (*Latin*) 'at this grave turning-point'; one of the
    commonest clichés of Latin prose
national poet of Ireland: Thomas Moore (1779–1852). Joyce is being
    ironic. Moore's sentimental verses about Ireland
    appealed to the English public but ignored realities
Firbolg: a race of early inhabitants of Ireland, in Gaelic
    literature the third race to invade and inhabit the
    country
Milesians: the fourth race of invaders who defeated the Fir-
    bolg
Davin: in real life Joyce's friend, George Clancy, who was
    later murdered by the Black and Tans when he was
    Mayor of Limerick
Michael Cusack: a blustering nationalist who founded the Gaelic
    Athletic Association in 1884
fenian: rebel republican
minding cool: defending as a full-back
caman: hurley-stick
handsel: lucky gift
Wolfe Tone: (1763–98) Irish patriot who helped to plan the
    French invasion of Ireland and was arrested in
    1798: he committed suicide in prison
the canonicals or the bellbordered ephod: priestly vestments
Pulcra sunt quae visa placent: (*Latin*) 'Those things are beautiful
    which give pleasure when looked at'
Bonum est in quod tendit appetitus: (*Latin*) 'The good is what our
    desire craves for'
Similiter atque senis baculus: (*Latin*) 'like an old man's walking-stick'
cliffs of Moher: they rise nearly seven hundred feet above the sea
    and extend five miles along the Atlantic coast in
    County Clare
Epictetus: the ancient Greek Stoic philosopher (*c.*55–135AD)
    who was born a slave, lame, and poor, and who
    preached the independence of the human mind of
    external circumstances, and that freedom is attained
    through patience and resignation: one must
    'endure and abstain'
**six principle men, peculiar people, seed and snake baptists, supralap-
sarian dogmatists:** these are all extreme dissenting sects holding eccen-
    tric views
insufflation: breathing on a person
imposition of hands: laying hands on people's heads

the procession of the Holy Ghost: the doctrine that the Holy Ghost *proceeds* from the Father and the Son

Per aspera ad astra: (*Latin*) 'Through hardships to the stars' (that is, 'The way to the stars is through hardships')

rounds of Kentish fire: an outburst of applause or noisy impatience: the expression refers to meetings held in Kent, 1828–9, in opposition to the Catholic Relief Bill

Leopardstown: the Dublin race-course

On a cloth untrue: from a song in *The Mikado*, an opera by W.S. Gilbert (1836–1911) and Sir Arthur Sullivan (1842–1900). Among imaginary torments is that of having to play billiards under these conditions

Ego habeo: 'I have'. Cranly and Stephen converse in a student lingo which uses Latin words in English order and with little respect for Latin grammar

Quod?: (student '*Latin*') 'What?'

– *Per pax universalis:* (student '*Latin*') 'For universal peace'

– *Credo ut vos sanguinarius... humore estis:* (student '*Latin*') 'I think you are a bloody liar, because your face shows you are in a damned bad mood'

– *Quis est in malo humore, ego aut vos?:* (student '*Latin*') 'Who's in a bad mood, me or you?'

MacCann: in real life Francis Sheehy Skeffington, later killed by the British in the Easter Rebellion of 1916

Stead: William Thomas Stead (1849–1912), an English journalist who fearlessly spoke his mind. He died in the *Titanic* disaster in 1912

John Anthony Collins: (1676–1729) English free-thinker

– *Pax super totum sanguinarium globum:* (student '*Latin*') 'Peace over the whole bloody world'

– *Nos ad manum ballum jocabimus:* (student '*Latin*') 'We are going to play handball'

Jean Jacques Rousseau: (1712–78) French philosopher

super spottum: (student '*Latin*') 'on the spot'

fianna: (*Irish*) soldiers

league class: Irish language class run by the Gaelic League which revived the language

stasis: stagnation

kinesis: motion

The Origin of Species: the study of natural evolution by Charles Darwin (1809–82)

Pange lingua gloriosi: a hymn celebrating the Last Supper. In modern hymn-books it begins, 'Now, my tongue, the mystery telling / Of the glorious Body sing'

Vexilla Regis: hymn celebrating Christ's crucifixion. In modern hymn-books it begins, 'The royal banners forward go'

Venantius Fortunatus: a sixth-century Italian, Bishop of Poitiers

Impleta sunt quae concinit . . . a ligno Deus: (*Latin*)

'Fulfilled is now what David told
In true prophetic song of old,
How God the heathen's king should be;
For God is reigning from the Tree'

are through the home civil: have passed the entry examination for the home civil service

the Indian: the examination for the Indian civil service

Lessing: Gothold Ephraim Lessing (1729–81), German literary critic and dramatist. His *Laocoon* is a work of aesthetic theory

– *Ego credo ut vita pauperum . . . in Liverpoolio*: (student '*Latin*') 'I believe the life of the poor is simply awful, simply bloody awful, in Liverpool'

Chapter 5, Section ii

Next morning Stephen wakes after an ecstatic dream in a mood of creative inspiration. It is like a divine incarnation in the virgin womb of the imagination. The verses of a villanelle addressed to Emma rise to his lips. He tears open a cigarette packet and begins to write his poem on the cardboard. Then he recalls memories of Emma—at musical evenings at her home and at a carnival ball where they danced together. The picture of her flirting with Father Moran is superimposed, and we learn how Stephen left his Irish class in high dudgeon as a consequence. The memory brushes the creative rapture away and shatters Emma's image amid memories of crude approaches by other girls. But Stephen recognises that his anger is itself a kind of homage. He sees Emma as a symbol of her country, turning from her true lover to whisper confessions in the ear of a priest of the Church rather than a priest of the imagination such as himself. For his own vocation is conceived in priestly terms. The bread of daily experience is transformed into the body of eternal life by the poet in his act of creation, just as it is by the priest at the altar in his act of consecration. The imagery of the Mass thus flows into his poem.

Stephen is conscious that he last wrote verse for Emma ten years ago after the memorable tram-ride. He decides not to send her the poem, but wonders whether she may be mysteriously aware of his devotion. Then he surrenders himself to a day-dream in which she responds lavishly to his physical desire as the words of the poem move through his brain.

COMMENTARY: This section is rich in irony. The vision of Emma sends the artist to lie on his bed and write poetry rather than to make contact with her. The poem that emerges is a highly artificial product of literary and religious verbalism. Rich in metaphor and rhetoric, persistent in rhythm, it surrounds Emma's image with the rising smoke of incense and praise, but there is no felt recollection of a real girl. Desire produces an orgy of sex-in-the-head, and devotion is expressed in the pre-digested imagery of Catholic liturgy. The poem is in no sense a communication. It is enjoyed by its author in private. Yet in his rare moments of self-criticism Stephen can still suspect that he has been unjust to Emma.

NOTES AND GLOSSARY:

Gabriel: the archangel who came to tell the Virgin Mary she was to be the mother of Christ, therefore a symbolic figure announcing an 'incarnation'

villanelle: a poem of five three-lined stanzas and a final four-lined stanza built around two rhymes only, with repetitions of the rhymes of the first stanza in subsequent stanzas (*aba aba aba aba aba abaa*), as in the full version of Stephen's poem

Gherardino da Borgo San Donnino: a thirteenth-century Franciscan who was imprisoned for heresy

the strange humiliation of her nature: menstruation

Chapter 5, Section iii

Stephen stands on the steps of the library watching the birds crying and circling above. Leaning on his ashplant, he is like an augur with his curved stick. The image of flight brings thoughts of Daedalus and of his own destiny. He goes inside the library and finds Cranly with Dixon, a medical student. The three of them leave the library, and outside they encounter a Dublin eccentric, 'the captain', reputed to be the offspring of aristocratic incest. They join a group of gossiping students. Temple, a little drunk, is talking pretentious nonsense about genealogies, and Cranly mocks him.

As Stephen watches them, Emma comes out of the library and, in response to Cranly's salutation, she bows to him and ignores Stephen. This sets Stephen brooding on Cranly's possible interest in her. Even so, the sight of Emma in the failing light evokes a strange inner delight, and he strolls away from the other students to indulge in reverie, first literary, then erotic. His conclusion is that he must dismiss her from his thoughts. He rejoins the group and eventually drags Cranly away on a walk.

Stephen discusses with Cranly the problem of his relationship with his mother. He has refused her tearful requests that he should go to confession and to Easter communion. By probing, Cranly elicits the main facts of Stephen's family situation, in particular what his mother must have suffered, and he urges Stephen to try to save her from further suffering since a mother's love is a reality compared to which ideas are futile. In reply Stephen tries to be clever about saints who have shrunk from their mother's embraces as dangerous sexual contacts. When Cranly probes him further, he concedes that he refuses the sacrament because he is not at all sure that the Church's teaching is false.

They have walked out into the suburbs. Stephen begins to feel decisively that his vocation is to go away and that his friendship with Cranly will not last. Cranly urges that there is no need for him to become an exile simply because of his anti-Catholic views, since many Catholics share his reservations. And he tries to suggest that Stephen's notion of 'unfettered freedom' is an unpractical one. In reply Stephen affirms his credo. He refuses to serve what he no longer believes in, whether it is home, fatherland, or Church. He is determined to express himself freely. Cranly takes Stephen's arm and speaks seriously, if enigmatically, of the possibility of life-long friendship. He seems to be offering it himself.

COMMENTARY: This section presents the snapping of various links which Stephen has with his homeland. As he focuses on the flight of the birds, it is the repeated 'sobs and reproaches' of his mother that their cries drown. The migratory lives of the birds call him from the supposedly ordered life of his homeland. In fact it is not very orderly in some respects. He recalls how Yeats's *Countess Cathleen* was received on the opening night of the national theatre, when students' boos and catcalls created pandemonium because they regarded the play as a 'libel on Ireland' and the work of an atheist. Stephen feels mentally severed from this cultural philistinism as he does from all the flippant student banter.

Emma's failure to greet him marks another severance. His suspicions of Cranly as a rival have the forced unreality of obsessive jealousy, like his suspicion of Father Moran. But more significant is the fact that Emma's beauty once more triggers off purely cerebral delight in thoughts of Elizabethan song-writers and images of erotic life in Stuart London. When Stephen finally, after de-lousing himself, consigns her in his mind to the care of some hygienic athlete who washes daily (presumably without his mother's assistance), the reader cannot but feel that she will be better off in such hands.

Cranly has hitherto been noted for taciturnity, but his cross-examination of Stephen on the subject of his mother is like the cross-examination of the priest after his earlier, formal 'confession'. Cranly's is the voice of common sense. We sympathise with his advice to Stephen to alleviate his mother's suffering. If he will not, he is surely guilty of inhumanity as well as of priggishness.

Throughout this section the idiom in which Stephen's inner reflections and his self-projections are expressed tends to be preciously 'poetic', and references to 'the heart of his weariness' and to his 'lonely heart' have a vaguely self-indulgent sentimentality. When he comes to define his personal creed and delivers his famous affirmations, 'I will not serve . . . ' and 'I do not fear to be alone . . . ' the rhetorical pretentiousness of this as yet untried young artist on the subject of himself is startlingly conceited.

NOTES AND GLOSSARY:

Cornelius Agrippa: (1486–1535), scholar and astrologer famous for his predictions, who was consulted by kings, including Henry VIII

Swedenborg: Emanuel Swedenborg (1688–1772), Swedish mystic and theosophical thinker

Thoth: Egyptian god of wisdom

Bend down your faces, Oona and Aleel . . . : lines from Yeats's play *The Countess Cathleen* performed at the opening of the Irish Literary Theatre in 1899. At a time of famine two demons persuade the Countess to sell her soul in order to buy food for the starving peasants. The play provoked protests of the kind indicated here

The Tablet: a Catholic theological journal

the Bantry gang: Timothy Healy (1855–1931) and his father-in-law Timothy Sullivan (1827–1914) from Bantry, County Cork, ostensibly supported Parnell but were not sorry to see him fall

Giraldus Cambrensis: Gerald of Wales (c. 1146–c. 1220) came to Ireland in 1184, and wrote *Topographia Hibernica*, an account of the geography and early history of Ireland

– Pernobilis et pervetusta familia: (*Latin*) 'a very noble and ancient family'

paulo post futurum: (*Latin*) an indication of something that is going to happen immediately

Dowland: John Dowland (1563–1626), English lutenist and composer

Byrd: William Byrd (1543–1623), royal organist and composer

Nash: Thomas Nash(e) (1567–1637), English playwright and critic

Cornelius a Lapide: (1567–1637) Flemish biblical scholar

Saint Augustine: Augustine of Hippo (354–430), one of the greatest theologians of the early Church

sugan:	rope
Siegfried:	the third of the four operas of Richard Wagner's (1813–83) cycle, *The Ring*
Pascal:	Blaise Pascal (1623–62), French theologian
Aloysius Gonzaga:	Italian Jesuit (1568–91) who was canonised in 1726
Suarez:	Francisco de Suarez (1548–1617), Spanish Jesuit theologian
– *Mulier cantat*:	(*Latin*) 'A woman is singing'
– *Et tu cum Jesu Galilaeo eras*:	(*Latin*) 'And you were with Jesus of Galilee', the challenge of the servant to St Peter which provoked his denial—from the Passiontide liturgy
proparoxyton:	a word accented on the penultimate syllable
Juan Mariana de Talavera:	(1536–1623) Spanish Jesuit theologian who justified tyrannicide

---

Chapter 5, Section iv

The last section of the book consists of scraps from Stephen's journal for the five weeks prior to his departure from Dublin. They touch briefly, and for the most part critically, on various friends such as Cranly, Lynch, Dixon, and Davin, on a further altercation with his mother, and on other passing experiences. A continuing thread of interest is provided by a series of references to Emma. On 23 March he notes that he has not seen her and that she is perhaps unwell. On 24 March he sees that she is not in the library, apparently not out and about yet, and questions himself whether he is worried about her health. On 2 April he sees her in a café, and on 6 April wonders whether she remembers the past as he does. She is in his thoughts again on 11 April, and finally on 15 April, when he meets her face to face in Grafton Steet, and treats her less than kindly. The realisation that he 'liked her today' only very briefly puts a brake on his new determination. For the next day's entry speaks of the call of distant places and the companionship of fellow-exiles. Finally he prepares to set out and prays for a blessing from his ancestor, Daedalus.

COMMENTARY: While the last section ended with a moving and deeply felt offer of life-long friendship by Cranly, this section begins with Stephen's cold and patronising dissection of his friend. By contrast the immense claims Stephen is prepared to make for himself become clear as he pictures a fanciful parallel between Cranly, the child of aged parents, and John the Baptist. As such, Cranly is the precursor of the Saviour (Stephen himself). The dream recorded on 25 March seems suggestive of the shadow of the dead Irish past which Stephen is going to shake off. The episode as a whole shows the artist taking over from the man. Friends are scarcely regarded as friends. Acquaintances and their doings become the material for self-conscious literary exercise. Human contacts seem to be less important than the fine phrases of the journal which they inspire. The seemingly disorganised jottings mirror the disconnected impressions with which the book opened, and suggest a second infancy.

NOTES AND GLOSSARY:

Elisabeth and Zachary: the aged parents of John the Baptist

locusts and wild honey: food on which John the Baptist lived in the desert

severed head: John the Baptist was beheaded by Herod

veronica: cloth on which the face of Christ was imprinted

Decollation: severance of the head from the body

Saint John at the Latin Gate: St John the Evangelist was miraculously liberated from persecutors by the Latin Gate of Rome

Bruno the Nolan: Giordano Bruno (1548–1600), born near Nola, an Italian philosopher, a Dominican who was charged with heresy and burnt at the stake

Blake: William Blake (1757–1827), English artist and poet

diorama: a pre-cinematic kind of illuminated scenic representation

Lepidus: a character in William Shakespeare's (1564–1616) *Antony and Cleopatra* (1607) who says, 'Your serpent of Egypt is bred now of your mud by the operation of your sun' (II.7.27–8)

Tara: the ancient capital of the kingdom of Ireland, in County Meath, a symbol of the nation's cultural and political identity

via **Holyhead:**   by way of exile, for Holyhead in Wales was the main British port of entry from Ireland

Michael Robartes remembers forgotten beauty ... faded from the world: Michael Robartes was a scholar-visionary with whom Yeats identified himself in his poetry. See 'He Remembers Forgotten Beauty', from *The Wind Among the Reeds* (1899):

> When my arms wrap you round I press
> my heart upon the loveliness
> that has long faded from the world.

Part 3

Commentary

The author's point of view

A Portrait of the Artist as a Young Man is autobiographical fiction and it is a study of growing up. Autobiographical fiction, in which the author uses the facts of his own life as basic narrative material, has a double interest for the reader. He is held by the story in the same way as he is held by the story in any other novel. He is also interested in the story because it reveals facts about the author's own life and character. Now if the reader is going to draw conclusions about the author's personal life and development, he must understand how much of the autobiographical fiction is accurately autobiographical and how much of it is pure fiction. Plainly if a writer simply wanted to leave behind him an accurate account of his own early life, he would write a pure autobiography (as many writers of novels have done). What are the motives, then, for choosing to write autobiographical fiction instead of pure autobiography? In some cases, it may be, autobiographical fiction is a mere device enabling the writer to represent real people under fictional names and so give himself a free hand at picturing publicly the men and women who surrounded him in his early days. Indeed he may wish to get his own back on some of them for their treatment of him. Autobiographical fiction may be used by the writer as a means of self-justification, proving to the world that he was right and others wrong in the struggles which marked his early days. For autobiographical fiction tends to be a record of struggle. The story of a person's growing up inevitably presents the individual's response to the pressures exerted upon him by those adults who try to mould him in a particular way and by those of his own generation who try to enlist him in fellowship with them. The hero has to make his choices, decide whose guidance to follow and whose to resist, and find his own way in life.

Joyce's *A Portrait* is clearly not direct, straightforward self-justification. Joyce certainly shows his hero struggling commendably against an adult world which in various ways tries to mould him in its own image, but he also shows emphatically how foolish, how immature, and indeed sometimes how wrong-headed his hero is. The reader is sometimes in deep sympathy with Stephen Dedalus's thoughts and feelings. At other times he is sharply critical of them or highly amused by them. Joyce has presented his hero in such a way that at one moment the reader shares his passionate anger and frustration at the way adults treat him, and at another moment the reader laughs at his vanity, his way of taking himself too seriously, and his indulgence in fanciful romantic dreams.

Many novelists have presented a hero or heroine with whom the reader can identify in sympathy throughout, and many novelists have presented a central character who is culpably wicked or laughably absurd in the reader's eyes; but only great novelists have managed to present a hero or heroine in such a way that the reader shares his or her feelings in deep sympathy and yet, at the same time, finds them often absurd and laughable. The double focus required to hold the hero in sympathy and also mock his foolishness is something which taxes the writer's resources to the full. Yet it is only necessary, say, to think of Jane Austen's (1775–1817) *Emma* (1815) to realise that there is nothing new in Joyce's achievement in this particular respect.

The literary device which enables the writer to achieve this double focus is *irony*. Irony is the device by which a writer conveys a meaning contrary to the expressed or surface meaning. It often contains an element of humour. Thus we can share in the deep stirrings of guilt aroused in Stephen by the retreat sermons and we can sympathise with his virtuous attempts to amend his life. But this does not prevent us from finding Father Arnall's accounts of torments in hell uproariously crude and ridiculous and Stephen's devices for leading a better life hilariously comic. What could be funnier than Stephen's method of disciplining his sense of touch by leaving part of his face and neck uncomfortably wet after washing? What could be funnier—yet what could be at the same time more awesomely heartfelt? It is the fusion of these two elements that constitutes irony; and irony here of a rarely powerful kind.

Nor is Stephen absurd only when he is taking himself rather too seriously as a penitent. He is absurd too when he is taking himself rather too seriously as a would-be artist. The rhetorical extravagance of the villanelle he writes for Emma Clery and the grandiloquent way in which he declares his artistic faith in conversation with Cranly have a kind of humourless solemnity that makes the reader smile. There are times too when Stephen's attitude and behaviour call for disapproval without even the solvent of laughter. His treatment of his mother seems to be unnecessarily cruel and the reader sympathises with Cranly's outspoken condemnation of Stephen in this respect. Joyce, indeed, was later so conscious of the way in which his hero comes under judgement that he said, 'I may have been too hard on that young man.'

Narrative method

Various methods of presentation are open to the writer of autobiographical fiction. He can write in the first person (in which case his book ought perhaps to be called 'fictional autobiography' rather than autobiographical fiction). Or he can write in the third person, as Joyce does. In either case he can present things as they are perceived through his hero's own eyes and through the hero's own mind instead of presenting them with impersonal detachment. This of course is Joyce's method.

The technique of presentation, whether of pure fiction or of autobiographical fiction, was transformed this century by writers such as Joyce himself. In particular the nineteenth-century technique of presenting passages of direct narration, inner reflection, description, and dialogue in a series of separate blocks was abandoned by many experimenters. Writers tried to move between outer narrative and inner investigation of characters' thoughts without the intrusion of connecting links. In the same way dialogue began to be interwoven with narrative or descriptive writing so that the reader might find himself attending at one and the same time to a conversation between characters and to what is going on in the mind of one of them. Clearly life itself is not divided up into chunks of talking and chunks of thinking isolated from external action. These processes are going on all the time, simultaneously. So it was in an attempt to equate the fictional world and the living world more convincingly that more flexible techniques of presentation began to be adopted.

Thus Joyce's novel does not begin: 'Stephen Dedalus was born in February 1882 in Rathgar, Dublin, the eldest son of Simon Dedalus . . .'. Nor does it proceed by clear and direct explanation of crucial stages in Stephen's story. There is no section beginning: 'When Stephen was six his parents decided to send him as a boarder to Clongowes Wood College, County Kildare . . .'. Instead of such direct statements, the first section begins with the voice of Stephen's father telling a bedtime story, and the second section begins with the description of a school playground swarming with boys. There is no recognisable authorial voice telling the reader the story, sharing a joke with him, giving the reader information which his characters do not have, or sometimes even addressing the reader as 'Reader'. All these are commonplace practices in eighteenth- and nineteenth-century fiction. The abandonment of such practices, and the attempt to float the reader alongside the characters in their own world, sharing their thoughts and feelings, and sensing through their eyes the impact of external events, has been the major development of twentieth-century fictional technique.

Does the development put too much strain on the reader? It is true that the reader has to exercise his imagination in order to keep his bearings. Joyce is careful to mark changes of scene clearly, but the reader has to keep his wits about him in order to follow the transitions that occur when Joyce moves from presenting the outer scene to presenting what is going on in Stephen's mind. For instance, in 1, iv Stephen is still wondering whether he really dare take his complaint against Father Dolan to the rector when he is already approaching the rector's door. 'He was walking down along the matting and he saw the door before him. It was impossible: he could not.' The first sentence is direct narration; the second is Stephen's thoughts. A novelist accepting earlier narrative conventions might have written: '"It was impossible," he told himself, "he could not".' But Joyce leaves the reader to sense through the rhythm of the words the movement from narration to inner reflection.

Style

The flexible method of presentation thus relies on omitting all avoidable instruction from author to reader, and therefore often conveys to the reader only obliquely who is thinking, who is speaking, what is happening, and where the scene is set. The absence of a recognisable authorial voice leaves opportunity for experimentation with style of a kind which nineteenth-century novelists did not attempt. For in most nineteenth-century novels you are listening directly either to the voice of the author or to the voices of his characters. When Joyce's novel opens you are listening to the voice of Mr Dedalus as remembered by Stephen from babyhood: when it closes you are listening to the 'voice' of Stephen as he commits his thoughts to paper as a young man. In between Joyce has run through a series of stylistic changes so as to match the style at every stage to Stephen's developing maturity and to the changes in his attitudes and feelings.

The earliest memories incorporate snatches of a bedtime story, a little song, and Dante's playful threat that the eagles will 'pull out his eyes' within a sequence of memories expressed with babyish inconsequentiality and simplicity ('That had the queer smell'). When Stephen is a young schoolboy at Clongowes, his thoughts and reflections are framed in short, plain sentences, direct, never complex in syntax, never decorated. They breathe the genuineness and innocence of the child as well as his mental immaturity ('He might die before his mother came.').

As the complexities of life impinge on Stephen's mind, whether in memories of the first response to the whiteness and softness of Eileen's hands or to the mysteries of the behaviour of other schoolboys and to the strangely odd or even cruel ways of the adults who teach him, the style becomes a little less spare and childish. Schoolboy expressions ('But Mr Harford was very decent and never got into a wax'), phrases from text-books ('the senate and the Roman people'), and snatches of remembered instruction ('the three patrons of holy youth—saint Stanislaus Kostka . . . ') occur to the mind, giving what is fundamentally still a simple boyish syntax a flavour highly appropriate and distinctive.

In the adolescent stage at Belvedere College, Stephen's reflections are expressed in a more sophisticated style which has acquired in its vocabulary and cadences the flavour of educational and literary influences now playing upon his mind ('he wondered why he bore no malice now to those who had tormented him'). In the religious crisis the extravagant rhetoric of the retreat sermons is reflected in the highly charged style of personal reflection ('His life seemed to have drawn near to eternity'). As Stephen goes through the agony of self-scrutiny and penitence, the phrasing and vocabulary of ecclesiastical exhortation, theological disputation, and books of spiritual guidance thread their way through his meditations.

In the final stage, when Stephen is a university student, the style acquires on the one hand, in Stephen's reflections and talk, a bookishness appropriate for a philosophically minded young man now feeding ravenously on the thought of great minds such as Aristotle and Aquinas, and on the other hand, in the cross-talk of students, a blend of mock-pedantry and irreverent crudity expressive of the undergraduate mentality. In the last section of all, which consists of passages from Stephen's diary, the style has become that of a conscious literary artist, one who has begun to discipline himself to a sharp selectivity in what he records, and to effect the record with the highly contrived 'artlessness' of one who is turning living experience into literature before it has time to grow cold.

Symbolism

Joyce's use of symbolism became crucial to his system of organising his material in *Ulysses*. He had experimented with symbolism in *Dubliners*. In *A Portrait* there is nothing so complex and thorough-going as the symbolism of *Ulysses*. Nevertheless the careful reader will detect that repeated use of certain words charges them with special significance. There is of course the ready-made symbolism that associates the cow with Ireland in the bedtime story, and the ready-made symbolism of national colours. Green is Ireland's colour, red is England's. At the Christmas party the red fire, the green flag on the cake, and the proximity of 'green ivy and red holly' suggest a harmony which is dissipated by the intrusion of politics. Again the rose is in some respects a symbol of England, and the Wars of the Roses are commemorated in the division into 'houses' at Clongowes school. Ireland is the green country. Stephen, as an infant, tries to sing mistakenly, 'the green rose blossoms', but he learns that 'you could not have a green rose'.

Since the cow is a symbol of Ireland, the reader can detect symbolic overtones in the account of how young Stephen thinks it would be pleasant to spend his life delivering milk to well-scrubbed cottages and smart homes. This is indeed a picture of settling down to Irish life in cosy comfort. But there is another side to the cow's environment, and Stephen is sickened by the 'foul green puddles and clots of liquid dung' the cow produces. Riding behind the trotting mare 'on the Rock Road' (this is the Blackrock Road; but the Rock is also a symbol for the Church) is not for him.

A recurrent motif throughout the book (and throughout Joyce's subsequent books) is provided by the symbol of water, in both its pleasant and unpleasant aspects, from the first wetting of the bed, through the soaking in the ditch at Clongowes and various references to lavatory water and washing in the kitchen, to the wading in the sea that precedes the sight of the transfigured girl. Exile involves flight over the sea. Crossing bridges is a symbol of decision. Stephen comes to a significant decision when he crosses the bridge to the Bull one way while Christian Brothers cross the other way to the kind of life on which he has turned his back. Imagery of flight is involved in references to Daedalus and Icarus, the birds, bats, and Lucifer. Study of Joyce's use of elementary descriptive words like 'cold' and 'hot', or 'white' and 'red', as well as his references to flowers, will reveal that his prose is shot through with thematic correspondences that link one part of the book with another and give artistic cohesion to the whole. Joyce's prose often has in this respect the texture of poetry.

There are many other symbolic themes that the student might investigate, for instance that of the labyrinthine searchings and uncertainties associated with walking corridors and the streets of Dublin, or those of darkness and light, blindness and sight, present at many points of the book—in the breaking of Stephen's glasses, in the sermons on hell, and in the conversation between Stephen and the dean of studies.

Epiphanies

The use of common objects such as bridges or common qualities such as hot and cold with special symbolic force is only one aspect of Joyce's artistic method, which is to enrich what is presented with heightened meaning. Joyce's way, as a writer, of responding to the full reality of a given object or event, of sensing what it reveals to the observer, was such that he used the word 'epiphany' for the experience. Technically the Epiphany is the Church's feast commemorating the coming of the Three Kings to worship the new-born Christ at Bethlehem. It is called the 'Showing forth of Christ to the gentiles'. An epiphany therefore shows forth the full reality of what is seen or observed. In *Stephen Hero* Stephen plans a book of epiphanies. 'By an epiphany he meant a sudden spiritual manifestation, whether in the vulgarity of speech or of gesture or in a memorable phase of the mind itself. He believed that it was for the man of letters to record these epiphanies with extreme care, seeing that they themselves are the most delicate and evanescent of moments.'

Joyce's method in *A Portrait* is to move from one experience to another in a series of epiphanies which reveal to Stephen the character of the world he lives in, the demands it is making, and the corresponding movements within himself towards acquiescence or rejection of it. In this sense the record is a series of epiphanies. They are rooted in commonplace events—like Mr Dedalus's recapitulation of the laughter with which Father Conmee and Father Dolan relished Stephen's protest over the unjust caning, the momentary intimacy with Emma on the steps of the last tram, the sight of the street name *Lotts* and the stink of horse urine, or the spectacle of a girl wading in the sea. These simple events achieve a momentousness in the full unveiling of their character to the developing mind of Stephen.

A study of Stephen

The reader must not identify Stephen with Joyce in every respect. For instance, Stephen is represented in his days at Clongowes Wood College as a timid boy, conscious of his smallness and weakness, who tries to avoid being involved in the rough and tumble of football. It is true that the young Joyce disliked fights, but he was keen on hurdling and cricket and won cups for his prowess. This practice of taking a certain aspect of his own character and intensifying and exaggerating it when picturing his *alter ego*, or second self, is typical of Joyce's method. The exaggerations often move Stephen a distance from the real Joyce. Who would guess from *A Portrait* that Joyce's cheerful disposition in youth earned him the nickname 'Sunny Jim'?

Stephen, then, is not simply a direct self-portrait. Indeed it is significant that Joyce called his book *A Portrait of the Artist* and not *Portrait of an Artist*. For Joyce was never content to record particular experiences for the sake of their interesting particularities. He wanted to achieve universality. Of his first book of short stories, *Dubliners*, he wrote: 'If I can get to the heart of Dublin, I can get to the heart of every city in the world. In the particular is contained the universal.' So we may assume that in studying the growth and development of Stephen Dedalus he was not exclusively concerned with getting to the heart of the young James Joyce or an imaginary equivalent, but in getting to the heart of the young artist as such.

In calling his hero 'Stephen Dedalus' Joyce consciously combined the name of the first Christian martyr and that of Daedalus, the legendary Athenian craftsman. Daedalus was credited with making statues that could move. He constructed the famous labyrinth at Crete. He made wings from feathers and wax so that he and his son Icarus could escape when Minos imprisoned them in the labyrinth. Icarus flew too near the sun so that the wax melted and he fell into the sea and was drowned. In giving his hero these names Joyce gave him symbolic status. The martyr suffering for his faith and the skilful, inventive artificer are joined in one person. Daedalus is significant both because he was a cunning craftsman giving life and complexity to his inventions and because he escaped imprisonment by the adventure of flight.

In the presentation of Stephen's infancy Joyce has compressed a series of references that hint at the larger issues in the child's future life. In fact infant memories are the acorn containing a promise in miniature of the future tree. The bedtime story sets the young hero in the road of life encountering a cow which is the symbol of the Ireland with which he will have to come to terms. The physical experience of finding relief and warmth in wetting the bed is followed by discomfort: this little miniature of delight seized that has to be paid for in pain, of ecstasy succeeded by sordidness or agony, sets the tone for many of the coming experiences. In the memory of Dante's brushes, representative of Davitt and Parnell, is foreshadowed the Irish political strife that is to ruin the Christmas party and provide a public background which Stephen, the university student, finds suffocating. The demand that the child should apologise or have his eyes pulled out foreshadows the later full-scale demand for repentance to escape the torments of hell.

The story of Stephen's development is the story of these pregnant contrasts and conflicts magnified. The child growing to young manhood has to face the impact on his individuality of the forces at large in the world he has entered. He is subject in turn to the pressures of family, of Church, and of his country, all trying to mould him in a particular way. The disillusionment experienced after bed-wetting is symptomatic of his maturer experience in this respect. The first separation from home at Clongowes is a move from the remembered warmth and cosiness of the family circle to a world of physical cold and discomfort and of emotional harassment by others, boys and masters. A chill caused by bullying brings him to the school sickroom in a shivering delirium. This is the first crisis of Chapter 1. The Christmas party at home to which he has looked forward, and which opens with promise of warmth, good cheer, and family friendliness, turns sour and then erupts into a violent slanging match because the public controversies of Irish history have impinged on the private scene. This is the second crisis of Chapter 1. The shock for Stephen is that Parnell is a hero, that priests are good and wise men, that these adults are all for Ireland, and yet tears and rage break up their conviviality. The third and last crisis of Chapter 1 is caused by the shock of Stephen's first encounter with flagrant injustice—injustice perpetrated by a priest in authority. Father

Dolan punishes him cruelly when he is innocent. The injustice stirs him to a brave and spirited bid for his rights. If Stephen is the loser, by sickness and by family discord, in the first two crises, he is victor in the third. The hero has protested in the face of the highest authority and has won his case. His individuality has triumphed over the iniquities of the system. This, in embryo, is the pattern of the artist's destiny.

In the period between Clongowes and Belvedere Stephen's development as a normal, healthy young boy who goes shopping with his uncle, and enjoys riding in the milkcart and playing on a farm, is accompanied by two stirrings of his inner life—one is the sickening foreknowledge of the family's financial troubles, which turns into embitterment when they move from the comfort of Blackrock to the cheerless house in the city: the other is the romantic dream life he creates for himself through reading *The Count of Monte Cristo* and picturing himself the partner of the lovely Mercedes. The first crisis of Chapter 2 is the shock of failure within himself. It occurs at the tram-stop with Emma Clery. Her eyes, her chatter, her way of coming to stand on the step beside him all seem to invite him to hold her and kiss her. But he does nothing; and the failure fills him with gloom. When he tries to write a poem to Emma, he empties the incident of reality and precision of detail and transforms it into a mistily conceived dream. As soon as the poem is written he goes to stare at himself—not to look for Emma.

The second crisis of Chapter 2 also involves self-dramatisation, this time in an actual theatrical performance on stage at Belvedere. A deep inner disturbance of desire, tenderness, and melancholy is focused on the belief that now, two years later, Emma is to watch him on stage with admiring eyes. The belief stimulates him to an excited and confident performance, after which he rushes out in wild expectation to his family, only to discover that Emma is not with them. The shock sends him running through the night streets of Dublin to a filthy corner where rankness and stench quench his inner agony. Interwoven with this record of emotional development Joyce traces the growing artistic confidence of Stephen's persistence in championing the rebel Byron against the respectable Tennyson.

The Cork visit serves to detach Stephen irrevocably from his father and his like. Tagging on behind his father, he recognises the hollowness of his garrulous bonhomie, is ashamed of the way he can be duped by an obsequious college servant, is embarrassed by his cheap flirtatiousness with barmaids, and is disgusted by his excessive drinking. Shame and humiliation open a chasm between his father's cronies and himself. The experience reinforces the humiliation already felt in his ambiguous status at Belvedere—a leading boy whose home background is one of squalor. And there is no escape to heroic self-confidence because he has become the victim of a restless inner lust and private orgies that fill him with self-loathing. There is an unbridgeable gap between the real world around him and what transpires in his own angry, impotent, dejected soul.

In the last section of the chapter Stephen makes a desperate attempt to re-establish order in his world and to rebuild effective relationships with his own family. The money prizes he has won for academic work are spent lavishly and recklessly on giving the family a taste of affluent living and turning himself into their banker and benefactor. When the money is gone, the whole attempt to stem briefly the tide of squalor and to come to terms with his family seems to have been futile. Meanwhile sexual desire is so unappeasable that he turns innocent girls seen by day into objects of imaginary lustful indulgence in his private dreams at night. There are still momentary day-dreams of fulfilment in the company of the idealised Mercedes; but the predominant urge is an animal demand to force some girl into sin and to take pride in it. In this mood he encounters the prostitute who takes him home. Thus the final crisis of Chapter 2 (like the final crisis of Chapter 1) ends in a kind of triumph, in that Stephen feels release, delight, and a new self-assurance when the prostitute moves into his arms.

The effect of sexual release upon Stephen is complex. His senses are repelled by the vulgarity of the brothels; he is conscious of his sinfulness, and yet too proud to pray, and afflicted with spiritual indifference. He is certainly not more open to others: on the contrary he finds himself scorning his school-fellows and simple worshippers. The aesthetic delight in the office of the Virgin Mary still captivates him. Somehow verbal sensuousness and ideal eroticism have become severed for him from the realities of living experience. In the same way interest in theological subtleties is now something isolated from religious faith and practice. Stephen has not found a way to self-fulfilment nor to love of others. The sexual act, which ought to be a means to both, has become one more experience for a would-be artist self-consciously inflating his own ego. It is in this deeply unsatisfied condition that Stephen is subjected to the retreat sermons.

The first crisis of this third chapter occurs when the rector announces the retreat and speaks of the sanctity, self-sacrifice, and heroic achievements of St Francis Xavier. Stephen feels an ominous withering of his heart. Father Arnall's previous contact with Stephen at Clongowes revives childhood memories, and his sermons are to thrust him back into a state of childlike submission and obedience. The introductory sermon and the sermons on death and judgement produce a second crisis, a sense of his shamelessness and foulness against which the thought of Emma stands in stark contrast. The shock of conscious guilt is resolved temporarily by another mental act of self-dramatisation when he pictures himself, hand in hand with Emma, being forgiven and comforted by the Virgin Mary. This romanticised day-dream is another absurdly extravagant product of the immature artistic mind. On the third day of the retreat the sermons revolve around the horrors of hell with an emphasis upon the physical torment of the senses and the moral and spiritual torments that accompany it. Designed to stir the conscience by stimulating fear, they constitute a burlesque of Catholic exhortation as absurd as Stephen's burlesque of artistic self-cultivation. Joyce emphasises the parallel by making Lucifer's slogan in rebellion against God (*non serviam*) Stephen's own slogan of commitment to his artistic vocation. Pride, the sin of Lucifer, is the sin which the egotistic young artist cannot recognise in himself. The final crisis of this chapter brings Stephen to a condition of terrified remorse, which is removed only when he makes his confession and receives absolution. Even in this act humility and sincerity are infected by self-dramatisation in the role of penitent. Like the previous chapters, this chapter too ends on a note of 'triumph'—again a romanticised triumph, that of the self-consciously cleansed young man receiving the sacrament in the joy of forgiveness.

In Stephen's next phase he cultivates his soul with elaborate devotional exercises, models his religious raptures on the romantic gestures represented in sacred art, and mortifies his senses with ingenious disciplines. All these practices have a degree of precious self-cultivation that is the reverse of true self-surrender. The persistent habit of self-dramatisation is evident in Stephen's various reflections on the director's suggestion that he might have a vocation to the priesthood. The first crisis of Chapter 4 comes when he weighs the call but suddenly realises that his own individuality can never surrender to the claims of such a calling. He has a 'pride of spirit' that makes him 'a being apart'. He must learn his own wisdom in his own way and face the world's snares. The decision to apply for a university place follows naturally. But there is a second brief crisis when Stephen meets a band of Christian Brothers who in their work and attitude have all the genuineness of devotion, humility, and charity which he himself lacks, and he feels ashamed and angry with himself in their proximity. This mood is resolved by the sudden assertion of his poetic self and his delight in words. The final crisis of the chapter, and the climax of the book, occurs when, dreaming of his urge to creative achievement as an artist, and feeling ready to shake off all that impedes him from following this calling, he sees a girl wading in the sea. Her beauty and her stillness fill him with rapture. Stephen exclaims, 'Heavenly God!' bringing his religious sense into a new context in response to the image of loveliness. The call of youth, beauty, and creativity throws him into an emotional ecstasy. The decisive choice of his life has been made.

The last chapter has thus the air of an epilogue. Yet the first section of it is the longest section in the book, and a good deal of experience is encompassed in Stephen's thoughts. The sordid scene at home is in stark contrast to the literary treasures stored in his mind. Though he scorns the pedantry of the lecture room, he relishes the magic of language with acute sensitivity. He has an off-hand attitude to the college time-table, and thinks but poorly of the dean of studies with whom he argues half-seriously, half-provocatively. He sits through the physics lecture in detachment. There is something of a show-down with fellow students in the entrance hall after the lecture, when he refuses to compromise with the sentimental aspirations of some of his companions and sign their petition. His cleverness at the expense of other people's earnest endeavours is bound to irritate and antagonise. Stephen manages to make himself unlovable by parading unpopular views uncompromisingly and doing so with calculated scorn. The charges of other students, that he lacks altruism and is a crank, win sympathy from the reader. Too often he seems to be spoiling for a fight, even with his genuine friends, such as Davin.

Stephen's long theoretical argument about the character of beauty is sandwiched between Davin's teasing reference to Emma and Lynch's whisper, 'Your beloved is here'. The contrast between the unrestrained verbalism of Stephen's talk about beauty and the equivocal, halting reservations that mark his attitude to a living woman is symptomatic of Stephen's failure to integrate thought and action. His head is full of theory about emotion and beauty, while his living experience of emotional commitment is confined to the brothel.

The thought that he may have misjudged Emma turns her in his mind, in a flash, into an epitome of natural gaiety and simplicity. When the poetic inspiration seizes him, his thought transfigures her into an object of devotion to be hymned exaltedly. The cry of the heart is transmuted into a precious rhetoric, rich and liturgical, but detached from the reality of the true relationship with Emma. Indeed Stephen's memories of her, now recalled, suggest a girl interested in him, ready to be responsive, doing her best to communicate, but being rebuffed by cool, oblique replies and the pose of isolation. Joyce's irony is never more subtle than here. Stephen's jealous anger at Emma's friendliness with Father Moran seems disproportionate. It seems to draw nourishment from his hatred of the Church and from his determination to make a priesthood of the artist's calling, a priesthood to which she ought to turn in frank confession. Stephen hovers between exaggerated condemnation of her as treacherous and exaggerated idealisation of her. Finally he conjures up her image as that of the voluptuous, yielding mistress at the point when the finished poem flows through his mind.

In the penultimate section of the book Stephen snaps the ties with home one after another. When he watches the birds and hears their cries it is the image of his mother's face and the sound of her weeping that they blot out. In deciding to fly, he is also consciously forsaking the Ireland of the vulgar barracking of Yeats's play. In conversation with Cranly he sums up his rebellious rejection of the Church and of the claims of his suffering mother. In relation both to his mother and to Emily Stephen manifests grave deficiency in human sympathy. The self-righteousness of his attitude is as priggish as the inflated language in which he presents his decision. In his own eyes his decisions are earth-shaking. He assumes to himself the importance of a future Beethoven or Shakespeare.

The notes from Stephen's diary suggest that within his divided being the conscious artist has taken over from the man of direct sympathy and unselfconscious action. The jottings have an artificial literary flavour. They show a young mind making art out of life. They sum up people and events with aphoristic dismissiveness. They employ archaisms, literary allusions, and clever-clever analogies in verbally discarding people who after all have loved Stephen—Cranly, Emma, his mother, his countrymen ('a race of clodhoppers'), and Davin. All are summarily treated as material for epigrammatic play by a super-mind. Meanwhile Stephen's own role is glamorised, his isolation, his spiritedness, and his resolve wrapped about with overtones of grandeur and heroism. The element of earnestness in his acceptance of the artistic vocation must not be ignored, but it is expressed here with a pretentiousness and flamboyance that cannot but raise a smile.

In the upshot Stephen emerges as a proud, rather anti-social person far too much wrapped up in himself. Cranly's question, 'Have you never loved anyone?' ought to touch a raw nerve. The lack of common humanity is surely Stephen's dominant weakness.

Other characters

Mr Dedalus

Mr Dedalus seems kindly enough when telling the bedtime story. At the Christmas party he is a generous host, a man with a lively sense of humour, a keen eye for the ridiculous, and a richly racy vocabulary. He is also a good mimic. An anti-clerical patriot, he has been deeply attached to Parnell. He makes an effort to avoid violent argument when his wife appeals for peace at the party and he tries to restore good-humour, but his command of vituperative language is eventually given full play at the clergy's expense. Mr Dedalus's financial troubles are hinted at in the Blackrock days and his rancour against his supposed enemies emerges, but as yet no blame is directly attached to himself. However, his snobbery, his social pretensions and his scorn of the riff-raff comes through in his talk about the Jesuits and the Christian Brothers. It is in the visit to Cork that Mr Dedalus is most fully portrayed. Here, through Stephen's mind, he is revealed as a sentimentaliser of his own past, a drunkard, a man with too much talk and too little responsibility. He is easily flattered, has phases of irrepressible and irrational joviality, and is absurdly proud of himself. Yet he is genuinely fond of Stephen, to whom he gives advice in ridiculous shallow clichés. He is quite happy for the family to batten on Stephen's prize money, it seems, for he gives no parental advice to husband it economically. By the time Stephen is a university student, Mr Dedalus's voice is heard in the background as that of a loud-mouthed family tyrant. When Cranly asks about Stephen's father's career, Stephen sums it up caustically, and Mr Dedalus is fully revealed.

Mrs Dedalus

Mrs Dedalus is only dimly realised as a character. She is remembered by Stephen from infancy as the person who smelt nice and played the piano for him to dance to. Repeatedly she is recalled as 'nice'—except when she cries. Stephen dreams of being kissed by her when he is at school, so plainly she is a fond mother. At the Christmas party she is the person who is most anxious to preserve the peace. She is a faithful Catholic, mistrustful of Stephen when he opts for the university, and deeply distressed by his rejection of the Church. The reader feels sorry for her as the wife of an irresponsible husband and the hard-pressed mother of a large family. She remains a background presence, a suffering mother roughly treated by her husband and by life. Stephen's refusal to alleviate her suffering adds to the reader's sense of her as a pathetic victim.

Dante

Dante is presented unsympathetically. Though she gives little Stephen cachous and teaches him interesting things about geography, she seems to have been sharper with him than his mother when he was naughty, threatening that the eagles would come and pull out his eyes if he failed to apologise. Her unthinking loyalty to the Church makes her rabidly hostile to Parnell and she is self-righteously provocative on the subject at the Christmas party. It is her bitterness that makes the full-scale row inevitable. She is the one who does not like Stephen to play with Eileen because she is a Protestant.

Mr Casey

Mr Casey is one of the most delightful studies in the book. He is the most attractive of the figures at the Christmas party. He has a sense of humour and knows how to talk to young children. He teases Stephen amiably about his neck and about his past. Stephen senses his goodness and his amiability. He feels 'affection' for him (a word not often used in reference to Stephen's relationships). It is his deep loyalty to Parnell and his horror at the Church's betrayal of him that eventually rouse him to a hysterical outburst against Dante's steady denigration of his hero, and then to tears.

Cranly

Stephen seems to choose as his university friends young men who can act as foils to himself. Cranly is recalled in his absence as an isolated head and face surmounted by ironlike black hair. He is above all a listener who can soak up Stephen's self-revelations with a seemingly placid unconcern. He rarely wastes words. He is direct, often clipped in speech; but when irritated capable of sudden outbursts of crude abuse. He assumes a kind of native superiority to the students around him. He does not make any effort to study. Yet he has an unpretentiousness against which Stephen's talk strikes as against a soundboard. He often maintains his 'listless silence', but occasionally interrupts with harsh comments. He exudes basic common sense. When Stephen has a serious personal issue to discuss—that of his relationship with his mother—he responds with solid home-truths. First he dissects Stephen's home situation in logical cross-examination, then he is fearlessly frank in telling Stephen what he ought to do. When they have thrashed things out together, he makes an offer of life-long friendship.

Davin

Davin is a peasant, an athlete, a romantic Irish nationalist fed from the cradle on Irish legend and hatred of England. His story of how he was apparently invited late one night to share the bed of a countrywoman and how he refused shows his integrity and simplicity. He will not let Stephen's taunts anger him. Stephen's private confessions upset him, and Stephen's refusal to be categorised mystifies him. 'Try to be one of us,' he pleads. He has simplified Irish history and the Irish problem in terms of heroic idealism and martyrdom in resistance to tyranny. There is something incongruous in the way Stephen warms to him, so different are they in outlook and temperament. Yet he is the only one to call Stephen 'Stevie'.

Part 4

Hints for study

Topics to select for detailed study

Since the whole book is the study of Stephen's development a full examination of the character of Stephen would require an essay on almost everything there is in the book. There are, however, many aspects of Stephen's development which can be examined separately.

1. Stephen's relationship with the family circle.
2. Stephen's relationship with other schoolboys at his school.
3. Stephen's relationship with other students at the university.
4. The effect of the Church on Stephen's personal development.
5. Stephen's response to the education given him at school and university.
6. The political issues touched on in *A Portrait* and Stephen's attitude to them.
7. Stephen's development in relation to the opposite sex.
8. Joyce's representation of the personality and temperament of the aspiring young artist.
9. The development of Stephen's interest in words and its influence upon his behaviour and his decisions.
10. What do we learn of Stephen from his various rebellions against authority?
11. Why does Stephen decide to leave Ireland?
12. What are the dislikeable aspects of Stephen's character?
13. Explain Stephen's aesthetic theory, and say what light it throws on his actual behaviour.

Other characters in *A Portrait* are seen primarily in terms of their influence upon Stephen. It is best to examine them in groups:

14. The family: Mr and Mrs Dedalus, Dante, Uncle Charles.
15. The clergy: Father Arnall, Father Dolan, the rector, the dean, the director.
16. The students: Cranly, Davin, Lynch, Temple, MacCann, Dixon.

There are also topics relating to literary technique:

17. Joyce's method of narration
18. Joyce's use of irony and humour.

19. Joyce's way of interweaving the outer scene and inner reflection.
20. Joyce's skill in matching style to different stages of the hero's growth and to different attitudes and moods of the characters.
21. Joyce's use of symbolism.

Selected quotations

Chapter 1

When you wet the bed first it is warm then it gets cold.

Pull out his eyes,
Apologize . . .

What was the right answer to the question? He had given two and still Wells laughed.

He might die before his mother came.

For pity's sake and for pity sake let us have no political discussion on this day of all days in the year.

They are the Lord's anointed, Dante said. They are an honour to their country.

— Sons of bitches! cried Mr Dedalus. When he was down they turned on him to betray him and rend him like rats in a sewer.

Eileen had long thin cool white hands too because she was a girl.

— Out here, Dedalus. Lazy little schemer. I see schemer in your face.

Chapter 2

In a vague way he understood that his father was in trouble and that this was the reason why he himself had not been sent back to Clongowes.

— She wants me to catch hold of her, he thought. That's why she came with me to the tram. I could easily catch hold of her when she comes up to my step: nobody is looking. I could hold her and kiss her.
   But he did neither . . .

— *I told them all at dinner about it and Father Dolan and I and all of us we all had a hearty laugh together over it. Ha! Ha! Ha!*

All day he had imagined a new meeting with her for he knew that she was to come to the play.

On the desk before him he read the word *Foetus* cut several times in the dark stained wood.

His childhood was dead or lost and with it his soul capable of simple joys, and he was drifting amid life like the barren shell of the moon.

In her arms he felt that he had suddenly become strong and fearless and sure of himself.

Chapter 3
Stephen's heart had withered up like a flower of the desert that feels the simoom coming from afar.

– Take hands, Stephen and Emma. It is a beautiful evening now in heaven. You have erred but you are always my children.

Theologians consider that it was the sin of pride, the sinful thought conceived in an instant: *non serviam: I will not serve*. That instant was his ruin.

God had allowed him to see the hell reserved for his sins: stinking, bestial, malignant, a hell of lecherous goatish fiends. For him! For him!

His soul was made fair and holy once more, holy and happy.

Chapter 4
To receive that call, Stephen, said the priest, is the greatest honour that the Almighty God can bestow upon a man.

His destiny was to be elusive of social or religious orders.

He passed from the trembling bridge onto firm land again.

Yes! Yes! Yes! He would create proudly out of the freedom and power of his soul, as the great artificer whose name he bore, a living thing, new and soaring and beautiful, impalpable, imperishable.

Her image had passed into his soul for ever.

Chapter 5
– Keep your icon. If we must have a Jesus let us have a legitimate Jesus.

I will not serve that in which I no longer believe, whether it call itself my home, my fatherland, or my church: and I will try to express myself in some mode of life or art as freely as I can and as wholly as I can, using for my defence the only arms I allow myself to use—silence, exile, and cunning.

Welcome, O life! I go to encounter for the millionth time the reality of experience and to forge in the smithy of my soul the uncreated conscience of my race.

Working on the text

The content and style of *A Portrait* are such that you may have to adopt a different method of preparing to write about it than you have used for other novels. To begin with, an autobiographical novel does not have a plot which ties all the strands of action together in a pattern. In a novel with a plot there is usually a group of characters surrounding the central character and entangled with him or her in various crucial actions. There is a crisis in the story at which the hero is put into a quandary or into danger, perhaps by the schemings of others, and a happy or a tragic outcome ensues when the difficulties have been surmounted or the wicked schemers have been unmasked, or else when the hero has been defeated. When there is a plot of that kind, the various characters can be examined for the part they play in it and what motivates them. The reader can compare what they think and say with what they do, and pass critical judgement on them.

An autobiographical novel does not have a group of characters who contrive or compete together to achieve a certain end, as Macbeth and Lady Macbeth plan to kill their king for his crown, and Malcolm and Macduff plan to bring the wicked assassins to justice. *A Portrait* is not the story of a scheme or a conspiracy or a young man's determination to marry the heroine. It is the story of a single person's growth and development from childhood to maturity. Such a story inevitably covers some twenty years. And during those twenty years the hero of this kind of book will inevitably be in contact with different groups of people at different stages of his development. There will be a family circle strongly influencing him as an infant, his school teachers and school-fellows strongly influencing him as a young schoolboy, and another lot of schoolmasters and school-friends influencing him as an older schoolboy. Last of all, there will be the lecturers and fellow-students strongly influencing him during his years at the university. So for the most part the reader cannot trace sustained courses of action by any character except the hero. The rest of the characters are, in a sense, all 'background' characters. They come into the story at certain points, do what they have to do in influencing the hero, and then fade out, except in so far as the hero may recall them to memory from time to time. So Dante seems like a crucial character in the first pages of the novel and Cranly is a crucial character in the last pages of the novel, but neither has a sustained role in the story of Stephen's twenty years. Father Arnall certainly plays a crucial role in influencing Stephen at a crisis in his life, but the character and private history of Father Arnall are of no interest to the reader apart from those few encounters at Clongowes and in the retreat at Belvedere when his story overlaps with Stephen's. In short, lots of characters in an autobiographical novel of this kind impinge on the hero briefly and then go their separate ways. The characters are important only for their influence upon the hero.

Joyce's novel presents another problem to the student who has been used to writing about the characters in other novels—what they look like, how they behave, and what their various temperamental peculiarities are. For Joyce does not describe his characters in the third person as other novelists might. He does not write: 'Mr Dedalus was a handsome, well-built man with black hair, a black beard and moustache, who wore a monocle. He had the air of a confident, breezy, knowing fellow, well pleased with himself but not all that pleased with the rest of mankind.' We do not get from Joyce accounts of this kind which would enable us to picture characters by piecing together the information he gives us here and there. For as author he scarcely tells us anything directly. He presents everything through the mind of Stephen. And Stephen's mind may not be all that reliable in registering the characters of those with whom he comes into contact. To begin with, for a large portion of the book Stephen is a child or a teenager, with a child's or a teenager's way of looking at things and of judging people.

If, therefore, you wished to give an account of the character of Mr Dedalus, you would have to comb the text, not for sentences telling you directly what kind of man he is, but for things he says himself that express his personality, for things other people say about him, and for things Stephen thinks about him.

Studying any aspect of any novel will always involve combing the text for passages that shed light on that particular aspect. But in this matter most novelists, especially earlier novelists, do much more of the work for you than Joyce does. Another novelist might have written, say, 'By the age of eight or nine Stephen was already a boy with a sensitive response to words and a prematurely romantic response to feminine beauty.' We are never told that, but we know that it is true. For instance, early in Chapter 1, Section iv, Stephen muses at Clongowes about the boy Boyle who is called 'Lady Boyle' by some of the others because of his habit of paring his nails. The thought of the boy's cared-for hands recalls Eileen's white hands. Stephen thinks of them as being like ivory and the phrase *Tower of Ivory* from the office of the Blessed Virgin Mary comes to his mind. Such phrases describing female beauty are not absurd for Stephen, as he understands they are for Protestants. Nor is the phrase *House of Gold* absurd when applied to the Virgin Mary, for he has seen Eileen's hair stream out like gold in the sunlight. We can learn a lot from carefully following the movement of Stephen's thought from sentence to sentence in a paragraph such as this one. We learn a lot of narrative detail from Stephen's recall of an occasion when Eileen put her hand into his pocket and then ran away from him—an episode which another writer might have described as it occurred, not as it was recollected by the boy later. The sexual overtones in this account of a childhood episode are obvious. From a single paragraph we glean a description of a memorable sunny day when Eileen was a little flirtatiously free with him, then scampered away from her own boldness as girls will, a knowledge of how such experiences are assimilated and recorded in Stephen's inquiring mind, and information about his way of linking boyhood responses to colourful language and to actual events. The paragraph illustrates what a concise writer Joyce often is. By his technique of recording a person's thoughts—a technique sometimes called 'interior monologue'—he can compress a great amount of narrative, descriptive, and psychological material into a brief compass. For if you dwell even longer on the paragraph it will occur to you that you have incidentally learned something more about the psychological divide between Catholic and Protestant in Ireland, and something more about the developing sensitivity to words and things in the early stages of the young artist's growth.

Combing the text and collecting material can be especially exciting and rewarding when you are dealing with a writer who presents it to you in such subtle and oblique ways.

The book as a whole: its structure

In dealing with *A Portrait* you cannot expect to remember the sequence of episodes as easily as you remember the order of events in a book with a well-planned plot. It is best to aid your memory by working out on paper the organisation of material in the succeeding chapters. As well as helping you in your studies such a summary will enable you to appreciate the careful construction of the novel. Each of the five chapters contains a number of sections. Sections are shaped so that in many cases they contain a crisis, or more than one crisis, in Stephen's experience. Each chapter ends with a climax that is a major turning-point in Stephen's development.

Your summary might be on these lines:

Chapter 1

Section i   Home. Infancy. Bedtime story. Song. Father. Mother. Dante. Eileen. Call to apologise

Section ii   Clongowes school. Football. Bullying (the ditch). Geography lesson. Chapel. Bed. Sickroom. Delirium

Section iii   Home. Christmas party. Mr Casey as guest. Talk of Parnell. Violent quarrel

Section iv   Clongowes. Broken glasses. Talk of boys' escapade. Lessons. Father Dolan canes Stephen unjustly. Stephen protests to the rector. Triumph (CLIMAX)

Chapter 2

Section i   Home. Blackrock. Company of Uncle Charles. Boyish play in gang. Rounds with the milkman. Deteriorating situation at home. Reads *Monte Cristo* and broods on Mercedes

Section ii   Removal. Dublin. Family visits. Party at Harold's Cross: effect of Emma: tram-ride. Poem to Emma. News of place at Belvedere and of how Stephen's protest at Clongowes was laughed at

Section iii   Belvedere. Play. Heron (flashback to challenge over who is best poet). Performance on stage. Emma not present. Stephen rushes off into city

Section iv   Visit to Cork. Train. Hotel. Queen's College. *Foetus* on desk. Father goes round pubs. Stephen feels isolated

Section v   Prize money. Stephen treats the family. Still restless and unsatisfied. Meets prostitute and goes with her (CLIMAX)

Chapter 3

Section i   School. Stephen uneasy. Retreat announced. Stephen wilts

Section ii   Introductory sermon stirs self-disgust (1st day). Sermons on death and judgment bring agony of shame temporarily alleviated by day-dream of forgiveness, hand in hand with Emma (2nd day).
Sermons on hell (3rd day) overwhelm Stephen

Section iii   Returns home in self-disgust and terror. Physically sick. Goes out to confess and is absolved. Finds relief and peace (CLIMAX)

Chapter 4

Section i   Stephen amends his life. Rigorous discipline of prayer and self-mortification

Section ii   Interview with director. Suggestion of vocation to priesthood. The idea attracts briefly, but Stephen rejects it

Section iii   Mr Dedalus enquires about university place. Stephen crosses bridge to the Bull (Christian Brothers). Envisages himself as artist and sees wading girl. Her image sends him into ecstasy (CLIMAX)

Chapter 5

Section i   Walk from home to university (thoughts of Cranly and Davin). Discussion with dean in physics theatre. Physics lecture. MacCann's petition. Talk with Cranly, Temple, and others. Walk with Lynch. Stephen expounds aesthetic theory. Catches sight of Emma

Section ii   Ecstatic dream. Stephen wakes to write poem to Emma

Section iii Stephen studies birds from library steps. Thoughts of flight. Contact with group of students. Emma greets Cranly, not Stephen. Walk with Cranly. Discussion of Stephen's relationship with mother. Stephen proclaims his faith.

Section iv Last jottings on friends and Emma. Preparations to leave (CLIMAX)

Specimen questions and model answers

1. Examine the development of Stephen's attitude to the opposite sex.

Joyce traces Stephen's sexual development with great care. As an infant Stephen is aware that his mother smells nicer than his father. As a small schoolboy he dreams of being kissed by her when sickness makes him long for home. As a young boy he imagines that he will marry his playmate Eileen when they grow up. It is Eileen's soft white hands and golden hair that first stir his romantic boyish notions of idealised womanhood; but the way she puts her hand in his pocket and runs away is the first instance of what his relations with attractive girls are to be. He lacks the maturity to take the initiative in practice or to respond when a girl takes the initiative. Instead he glamorises the experience in words. For Stephen the mental romanticisation of love is one thing; the experience of living girls is another thing. The two experiences are never brought into harmony. Thus Stephen indulges romantic dreams about Dumas' Mercedes, but it is significant that he pictures himself grandly rejecting her approaches because she had earlier slighted his love. The pose of grand, offended isolation is all too attractive to him.

The first fully recognisable sexual encounter occurs when Stephen goes to the party at Harold's Cross. He withdraws from the other children, relishing his isolation, while Emma glances repeatedly and invitingly in his direction. She rouses him to feverish excitement, and after the party she goes with him to the tram-stop. They stand on the tram steps, he a step above hers, and as they talk she keeps coming up to join him on his step. He knows that she is making an offer; he also knows that the experience is like the occasion when Eileen ran laughing away from him. But for all his sense of her beauty and his knowledge that she is ready to be held and kissed, he does nothing. The failure depresses him. Then, next day, he begins to turn the whole experience —which should have had a living climax—into a literary matter. He tries to write a poem to Emma and consciously brushes the realities of the scene out of his mind. He turns the memory into an exercise in vague, conventionalised poetic verbalism. And after that he goes and stares at himself in the mirror. His own pose as a romantic poet is more fascinating to him than the living girl who has inspired it.

Two years later, on the occasion of the school play, Stephen works himself up into an excited romantic mood in the belief that he will meet Emma after she has seen the play. Once more the devotion is an uncommunicated obsession based symbolically on a dramatic performance. After the play, in which he excels in the world of imaginary self-projection, Emma is nowhere to be found and he is plunged into despair. Stephen's awakening sexuality, then, is blocked off from real human relationships and diverted into romantic dreams fed by his reading. *The Count of Monte Cristo* and Bulwer Lytton's *The Lady of Lyons* supply him with imaginary situations of romantic love. As a result, his suppressed physical urges produce a perverted urge to sin and to force someone else into sin. The consequence is that when he meets a prostitute in the street one night, he is readily lured to her room and as she takes the initiative and embraces him he finds not only relief from the urges of lust but a new self-assurance.

For a time sexual experience with prostitutes runs alongside his romantic adoration of the Virgin Mary until the retreat sermons convince him of his wickedness and he repents. We are not told whether, after his loss of faith, he returned to the habit of visiting prostitutes. But clearly he fails to make a connection between the romantic sexuality in his mind, which is stirred so deeply by the sight of the wading girl, and the life of real contact with women. The wading girl becomes an ideal to move the artist to creative dedication. Real human relationship is not involved.

The fitful references to Emma in the last chapter of the book suggest a very slight interest in living beauty compared to the passionate intellectual interest in the theory of beauty. Though Stephen chooses to imagine that Emma flirts with Father Moran, the sight of her by the library door stirs the thought that she may be innocent and there is another uprush of emotion—but it all goes into dreams and words, not into real contact with her. He writes an extravagantly rhetorical poem to her and pictures himself, the priest of the imagination, listening to her confession. Stephen's mental life and his concept of himself as the heroic lonely artist are plainly incompatible with sympathetic understanding of others. He indulges the notion that Emma is consciously rebuffing him and that Cranly is pursuing her when she ignores him outside the library. In consequence he mentally washes his hands of her. 'Let her go and be damned.' But the reader lacks evidence to know how far Stephen is deceiving himself. Indeed the last references to Emma in his diary give the impression of a girl who is trying hard to make contact with him. She wants to know why she sees so little of him and whether he is writing poems, and his reply is a churlish rebuff calculated to embarrass her. Stephen's final observation, 'I liked her and it seems a new feeling to me', is one of the most revealing sentences in the book. Stephen has expressed a liking for another human being and has conceded that the feeling is a new one to him.

Stephen's relationships with girls suffer from his egotism. He cultivates an image of himself as an isolated artist. His sexual instincts are satisfied with prostitutes. His romantic yearnings are channelled into poems and day-dreams.

---

2. Why does Stephen choose exile from his native land?

Stephen chooses exile from his native land partly because he cannot come to terms with the authorities that hold its people in their grip. Indeed his mental development is achieved through a series of struggles with authority as it is represented in the home environment from which he ultimately decides to flee. His sense of injustice is stirred when he is a young schoolboy. When Wells asks him if he kisses his mother at bedtime, he discovers that whether he should say Yes or No he is laughed at. Wells has already shouldered him into the ditch, and this first experience of school bullying makes him ill. Christmas at home, which is expected to be all warmth and friendship and happiness after the chilly misery at school, turns out to be a time of angry political quarrels among adults who are all supposed to be devoted to Ireland. When Stephen returns to school, after suffering the misfortune of having his glasses broken he suffers the injustice of being punished for it. Priests are supposed to be good, he thinks, but they get angry and behave cruelly. To make things worse, he later discovers that bold protest against injustices becomes a subject for laughter among those responsible for the injustice.

The undermining of Stephen's confidence in the moral authority of the powers-that-be at school is accompanied by the undermining of his respect for his own father. The visit to Cork reveals Mr Dedalus as a boastful, flattery-loving gas-bag and drunkard, drinking and boasting while all the time his affairs are deteriorating and the home is getting more squalid. Stephen's boyish attempt, when he gets his prize money, to stem the tide of sordid poverty that seems to be sweeping over his family proves absurdly inadequate. His attempt, after confession, to remodel himself on the pattern of perfection taught by the Church, leads to extravagant feats of self-discipline that deny his most powerful aspirations towards life and beauty. When the suggestion is made that he should consider vocation to the priesthood, an instinctive inner conviction assures him that his future cannot be in subjection to an ordered system like that of the Church. The vision of the wading girl stirs the religious outburst, 'Heavenly God!' and we recognise in the way the landscape calls up in him poetic phrases that satisfy his thirst for harmony between the outer world and his inner emotional life, that he is a future artist not a future priest.

It is from a sordid scene at home and past the mad cries from a nunnery that Stephen makes his symbolic progress across Dublin to the university, where study opens up a world of exciting philosophical thought. But even here there is no prospect of ultimate life-long satisfaction. For the university teachers are seen as limited and unimaginative, and the students' enthusiasm is stirred by causes with which Stephen cannot sympathise. The idealistic support for the Czar's peace initiative strikes him as sentimental. He feels unable to commit himself to corporate demands or protests. The enthusiasm of students such as Davin for the cause of national independence, the revival of native culture, and enmity against England seem to require a commitment that mortgages life in advance of living it. Stephen senses his own Irish inheritance, not as a great blessing, but as a series of fetters imposed by history willy-nilly on his generation. Moreover he knows from the past that Irish nationalist movements tend to lead, not to victorious achievements by the leaders, but to their betrayal and martyring.

Stephen himself demands of life, above all, freedom in which he can work creatively as an artist. Closely associated with the demand for freedom is his sensitive responsiveness to beauty in the spoken and written word. He has found in his home an increasing sordidness and crudity that are the antithesis of beauty. He has found in the Church a cruelty hostile to justice and freedom, for the caning with the pandybat at Clongowes is of a piece with the horrendous torments pictured in Father Arnall's sermons as the future eternal lot of millions of fellow human beings. He has found in the political life of Ireland a collection of inherited attitudes and passions that embitter family relationships, that turn young students into obsessed fanatics, and that claim people's thoughts and energies before they have had time to develop their own individualities.

The upshot is that Stephen turns the rebellious slogan of Lucifer, in turning against God, 'I will not serve', into his own motto in rejecting the demands of home, fatherland, and Church, and dedicating himself to the task of expressing himself freely as an artist.

The decision takes shape in his mind in association with thoughts of the career of his mythical 'ancestor', Daedalus, who found escape in flight from imprisonment in a labyrinth. Stephen has often trod the maze of Dublin streets seeking escape of one kind or another, whether in the confessional or in a brothel. Only when he crosses a bridge to an island and stares out to sea does he glimpse the vision of true fulfilment. He cannot find it without flight.

3. Exemplify Joyce's use of humour and irony.

Irish writers are often noted both for their irony and for their humour, and Joyce uses a great deal of comic irony in *A Portrait of the Artist as a Young Man*. Irony is not always comic. It is ironic when a hero kills his own son not knowing who he is, but the irony is wholly tragic. It is ironic that a Christmas party meant to be the occasion of peace and goodwill should turn into a violent family row and a virulent exchange of abuse. It is sad too, and Stephen feels its sadness; but it also has its comic side. We smile when Dante, a rather self-important person conscious of her own dignity, is turned into a screaming virago quivering with rage, and when Mr Dedalus lets off steam in comic abuse of Church dignitaries.

Humorous irony in literature often revolves around the way self-important or pretentious people are brought down to earth with a bang. In *A Portrait* Stephen is the main concern of the author and he happens to be himself a rather self-important and pretentious person. Joyce often punctures his pretentiousness—not in his own eyes and not in the eyes of other characters, but in the reader's eyes. For instance, when Stephen makes his righteous protest against being unjustly punished by Father Dolan, he pictures himself like some great public figure of history standing up against tyranny. The little boy appealing to his headmaster sees himself in this grand light and, when his protest has been accepted, he resolves not to take advantage personally of his vanquished foe, and the reader smiles indulgently at his childish self-importance.

Stephen's romantic dreams often evoke an indulgent smile in the reader. He pictures himself, at the end of a long series of heroic adventures, proudly declining Mercedes's offer of grapes. When he helps to lead a gang of boys, he sets himself apart from the others by not adopting their symbols and uniform, because he has read that Napoleon also remained unadorned. These comic comparisons made by the little boy are rich in ironic humour.

These are of course the kind of imaginative exaggerations which are common to childhood. But they lead to less usual extravagances in the growing artist. When a boy sits down, as Stephen does, to write a poem to a girl, begins it by imitating Lord Byron's habit of entitling such poems, but finishes up staring at himself admiringly in a mirror, the gap between supposed intention and reality is wide. Later Stephen imagines a stage triumph before Emma's eyes and rushes off to claim his due of feminine admiration only to finish up in a squalid corner of the city amid the smell of horse urine. These contrasts are the stuff of irony. So is the contrast between the boy's glamorous dreams of himself as a romantic lover and the actual experience to which they lead in a city brothel.

The retreat sermons are a sustained ironic piece, and the irony this time is not primarily at the expense of the hero but of the Catholic Church and its clergy. The sermons seem to start reasonably enough but gradually become a burlesque of the kind of teaching given in retreats. That is to say, they follow the course of traditional moral exhortation but push the examples to such an extreme that the effect is laughable. A further irony is that the ingenuity with which torments are seemingly devised by God and the relish with which they are described by the priest are not congruous with notions of a loving God and a religion of love. Equally ironic is the meticulous and literal way in which Stephen tries to mortify his senses and discipline his mind. The sermons plainly have had on him the maximum effect intended by the priest. Now that Stephen is repentant the reader naturally warms to him in sympathy, but he has to smile at the degree of vanity and self-centredness Stephen shows in trying to model himself anew.

In some respects the irony at Stephen's expense is sharpest in the last chapter of the book. For when he becomes a student his aspirations aim higher and higher, and are grandiloquently expressed. The contrast between these aspirations and the reality around him is often laughably sharp. At the end of Chapter 4, for instance, Stephen has enjoyed raptures expressed in language of ecstatic lyrical beauty. At the beginning of Chapter 5 he is drinking watery tea and chewing crusts of fried bread at a dirty kitchen table. Joyce puts these two episodes together with comic intent. Again Stephen propounds his high doctrine of beauty to fellow-students who, for the most part, have only crude and vulgar witticisms to contribute to the conversation.

Stephen dismisses real living beauty from his mind in order to theorise about beauty with his intellect. Inspired suddenly by Emma's beauty, he writes a poem in a language utterly removed from the idiom of living human relationships. It is poetry so precious and high-falutin that real feeling is left out. The irony of hymning a girl so richly in secret and virtually snubbing her when she makes natural friendly approaches is both amusing and rather sad. Not for the first time the reader wants to shake Stephen to try to knock some sense into him; above all to make him a little more human.

---

4. Examine the structure of Joyce's *A Portrait*

Joyce's *A Portrait* is constructed of five chapters, each containing a number of sections. The episodes which make up the succeeding sections tend to be shaped around crises that are milestones in Stephen's development. These crises either bring him up against some eventuality that reveals his weakness and the world's hostility or they give him a taste of fulfilment and success.

The first section of Chapter 1 ends with Stephen hiding guiltily under the table while adults demand that he should apologise, and threaten terrible punishment. After this defeat at home the second section brings an experience of defeat at school. Bullying brings him to the sickroom and to delirious dreams. The third section culminates in the row at the Christmas party. All these crises are negative experiences for Stephen, and there is a worse one to follow in Section iv when he is cruelly caned, though innocent. But this time Stephen reacts positively, makes his protest, and turns defeat into triumph. He is held shoulder-high by his school-fellows.

The first two sections of Chapter 2 present a violent contrast. The first section shows Stephen escaping from the deteriorating situation at home into romantic day-dreams. The crisis shows him magically trans-figured into a fearless and confident hero, rebuffing Mercedes. But in real life two defeats follow in Section ii. He fails miserably to respond to Emma's approaches on the tram, and he learns that his protest at Clongowes was an hilarious joke to Father Conmee and Father Dolan. The contrast between success in the imaginary world and defeat in the real world is pursued further in Section iii. A flashback shows Stephen heroically refusing to conform in his choice of the best poet. This is a victory of the spirit in the literary sphere. Likewise Stephen channels all his emotional restlessness into a fine stage performance only to find that Emma is not there to receive him with admiration afterwards. Triumph in the dramatic world is turned into defeat in the real world.

In Section iv, during the visit to Cork, Stephen experiences a series of minor inner crises which cumulatively erode his respect for his father and his sense of community with others. An attempt is made to retrieve the family situation by means of Stephen's prize money in Section v, but it fails dismally and the pressures of unsatisfied desire drive him into the arms of a prostitute. In the sense that this experience brings temporary relief and self-assurance to Stephen, the climax of the chapter is once more a 'triumph' for him.

It is, however, a total perversion of the romantic idealism which seeks expression in living experience. Thus Chapter 3 moves directly through four crises in which the call to repentance intrudes with increasing force on Stephen's now restless, moody, and morally dis-oriented condition. He hears the retreat announced and St Francis Xavier's sanctity extolled, and his heart withers within him. The introductory sermon, the sermons on death and judgement, and the sermons on hell produce crises of escalating self-disgust and terror until finally Stephen is driven to confess. As in previous chapters the climax is thus a 'triumph' in that it brings immediate release and peace.

Chapter 4 traces the struggle and resolution over the question whether Stephen should become a priest. Crisis points in the three sections occur as he weighs the attractions of priestly vocation and rejects them, as he finds himself crossing a bridge in the opposite direction from dedicated Christian Brothers, and as he conjures up a vision of himself as artist soaring aloft like Daedalus and finds it complemented in the spectacle of the wading girl whose appearance is transfused with beauty. Stephen's vocation is now clear.

The climactic ending to Chapter 4 decisively sets the course of Stephen's career. His growing-up is completed in the sense that, as a student, he does not mature through a series of further defeats and successes, but works out for himself his theory of art and the claims of his vocation. For this reason the structure of the last chapter is less dramatic and more reflective. Though Stephen is involved in conflict—with Irish nationalists and other political activists, for instance—he is not under trial. There is no crisis suggesting that Stephen may throw in his lot with Davin or MacCann. He stands his ground as one above the struggle. Even the romantic dream of Emma and the rapturous poem she inspires do not make the reader suspect that Stephen might after all settle down and bring up a family in Dublin. In this chapter the student mind turns the stuff of life into talk and theory and banter, while for Stephen the issues which prevent him from coming to terms with Ireland are clarified one by one.

Part 5

Suggestions for further reading

The text

A Portrait of the Artist as a Young Man, text, criticism, and notes, edited by Chester G. Anderson, Viking, New York, 1967.
A Portrait of the Artist as a Young Man, Modern Novels Series, Heinemann Educational, London, 1979.
A Portrait of the Artist as a Young Man, Panther paperback, Granada, London, 1977.

Other works by James Joyce

Dubliners, Grant Richards, London, 1914.
Stephen Hero, ed. Theodore Spencer, Jonathan Cape, London, 1944; revised by J.J. Slocum and H. Cahoon, Jonathan Cape, London, 1956.
Ulysses, Shakespeare and Co., Paris, 1922; John Lane, The Bodley Head, London, 1937.
Finnegans Wake, Faber, London, 1937.
Selected Letters of James Joyce, ed. Richard Ellman, Faber, London, 1976.
James Joyce: Critical Writings, ed. E. Mason and R. Ellmann, Faber, London, 1959.

General reading

ANDERSON, CHESTER G.: *James Joyce and His World*, Thames & Hudson, London, 1967. An attractive illustrated introduction to Joyce's life and work.
BIDWELL, BRUCE, and HEFFER, LINDA: *Joycean Way. A Topographical Guide to Dubliners and A Portrait of the Artist*, Wolfhound Press, Dublin, 1982.
BLAMIRES, HARRY: *Twentieth-Century English Literature* (The Macmillan History of Literature), Macmillan, London, 1982. A book which puts major writers of our century into their historic context.

BLAMIRES, HARRY: *Studying James Joyce*, York Handbooks, Longman, Harlow, 1986.

BLAMIRES, HARRY: *The Bloomsday Book: A Guide through Joyce's 'Ulysses'*, University Paperbacks, Methuen, London, 1966. A book designed to help the reader to a quick understanding of Joyce's masterpiece.

BOLT, SYDNEY: *A Preface to James Joyce*, Longman, London, 1981. A useful introductory book for the student.

ELLMAN, RICHARD: *James Joyce*, Oxford University Press, 1959, revised 1982. This standard biography of Joyce is one of the great literary biographies of our age.

*GIFFORD, DON: *Joyce Annotated: Notes for Dubliners and A Portrait*, University of California Press, Berkeley/Los Angeles/London, 1982; revised and enlarged from *Notes for Dubliners and A Portrait*, Dutton, New York, 1967.

JEFFARES, A.N.: *Anglo-Irish Literature* (The Macmillan History of Literature), Macmillan, London, 1982. A book which places modern Irish writers in their historic Irish context.

SCHOLES, R.E. and KAIN, R.M.: *The Workshop of Daedalus: James Joyce and the Materials for APYM*, Northwestern University Press, Evanston, Illinois, 1965.

---

* Don Gifford's book of notes is a mine of interesting material and sheds light on the problems raised by Joyce's text. The author of these Notes has been indebted to this book at many points.

The author of these notes

HARRY BLAMIRES is a graduate of the University of Oxford, where he studied English Language and Literature. He spent a large part of his teaching life as Head of the English Department at King Alfred's College, Winchester, but retired early to turn to full-time writing in 1976. His publications include works of fiction and theology as well as literary history and critical books on James Joyce, T.S. Eliot, and Milton. His *Twentieth Century English Literature*, Macmillan, London, 1982, is a volume in the Macmillan History of Literature (ed. A.N. Jeffares). He has recently edited *A Guide to Twentieth-Century Literature in English*, Methuen, London, 1983, to which he has himself contributed the articles on the writers of the United Kingdom and Ireland. His popular survey, *A Short History of English Literature*, Methuen, London, has been expanded and updated in a Revised Edition (1984).

York Notes: list of titles

CHINUA ACHEBE
A Man of the People
Arrow of God
Things Fall Apart

EDWARD ALBEE
Who's Afraid of Virginia Woolf?

ELECHI AMADI
The Concubine

ANONYMOUS
Beowulf
Everyman

JOHN ARDEN
Serjeant Musgrave's Dance

AYI KWEI ARMAH
The Beautyful Ones Are Not Yet Born

W. H. AUDEN
Selected Poems

JANE AUSTEN
Emma
Mansfield Park
Northanger Abbey
Persuasion
Pride and Prejudice
Sense and Sensibility

HONORÉ DE BALZAC
Le Père Goriot

SAMUEL BECKETT
Waiting for Godot

SAUL BELLOW
Henderson, The Rain King

ARNOLD BENNETT
Anna of the Five Towns

WILLIAM BLAKE
Songs of Innocence, Songs of Experience

ROBERT BOLT
A Man For All Seasons

ANNE BRONTË
The Tenant of Wildfell Hall

CHARLOTTE BRONTË
Jane Eyre

EMILY BRONTË
Wuthering Heights

ROBERT BROWNING
Men and Women

JOHN BUCHAN
The Thirty-Nine Steps

JOHN BUNYAN
The Pilgrim's Progress

BYRON
Selected Poems

ALBERT CAMUS
L'Etranger (The Outsider)

GEOFFREY CHAUCER
Prologue to the Canterbury Tales
The Clerk's Tale
The Franklin's Tale
The Knight's Tale
The Merchant's Tale
The Miller's Tale
The Nun's Priest's Tale
The Pardoner's Tale
The Wife of Bath's Tale
Troilus and Criseyde

ANTON CHEKOV
The Cherry Orchard

SAMUEL TAYLOR COLERIDGE
Selected Poems

WILKIE COLLINS
The Moonstone
The Woman in White

SIR ARTHUR CONAN DOYLE
The Hound of the Baskervilles

WILLIAM CONGREVE
The Way of the World

JOSEPH CONRAD
Heart of Darkness
Lord Jim
Nostromo
The Secret Agent
Victory
Youth and *Typhoon*

STEPHEN CRANE
The Red Badge of Courage

BRUCE DAWE
Selected Poems

WALTER DE LA MARE
Selected Poems

DANIEL DEFOE
A Journal of the Plague Year
Moll Flanders
Robinson Crusoe

CHARLES DICKENS
A Tale of Two Cities
Bleak House
David Copperfield
Dombey and Son
Great Expectations
Hard Times
Little Dorrit
Nicholas Nickleby
Oliver Twist
Our Mutual Friend
The Pickwick Papers

EMILY DICKINSON
Selected Poems

JOHN DONNE
Selected Poems

THEODORE DREISER
Sister Carrie

GEORGE ELIOT
Adam Bede
Middlemarch
Silas Marner
The Mill on the Floss

T. S. ELIOT
Four Quartets
Murder in the Cathedral
Selected Poems
The Cocktail Party
The Waste Land

J. G. FARRELL
The Siege of Krishnapur

GEORGE FARQUHAR
The Beaux Stratagem

WILLIAM FAULKNER
Absalom, Absalom!
As I Lay Dying
Go Down, Moses
The Sound and the Fury

HENRY FIELDING
Joseph Andrews
Tom Jones

F. SCOTT FITZGERALD
Tender is the Night
The Great Gatsby

E. M. FORSTER
A Passage to India
Howards End

ATHOL FUGARD
Selected Plays

JOHN GALSWORTHY
Strife

MRS GASKELL
North and South

WILLIAM GOLDING
Lord of the Flies
The Inheritors
The Spire

OLIVER GOLDSMITH
She Stoops to Conquer
The Vicar of Wakefield

ROBERT GRAVES
Goodbye to All That

GRAHAM GREENE
Brighton Rock
The Heart of the Matter
The Power and the Glory

THOMAS HARDY
Far from the Madding Crowd
Jude the Obscure
Selected Poems
Tess of the D'Urbervilles
The Mayor of Casterbridge
The Return of the Native
The Trumpet Major
The Woodlanders
Under the Greenwood Tree

L. P. HARTLEY
The Go-Between
The Shrimp and the Anemone

NATHANIEL HAWTHORNE
The Scarlet Letter

SEAMUS HEANEY
Selected Poems

JOSEPH HELLER
Catch-22

ERNEST HEMINGWAY
A Farewell to Arms
For Whom the Bell Tolls
The African Stories
The Old Man and the Sea

GEORGE HERBERT
Selected Poems

HERMANN HESSE
Steppenwolf

BARRY HINES
Kes

HOMER
The Iliad
The Odyssey

ANTHONY HOPE
The Prisoner of Zenda

GERARD MANLEY HOPKINS
Selected Poems

WILLIAM DEAN HOWELLS
The Rise of Silas Lapham

RICHARD HUGHES
A High Wind in Jamaica

THOMAS HUGHES
Tom Brown's Schooldays

ALDOUS HUXLEY
Brave New World

HENRIK IBSEN
A Doll's House
Ghosts
Hedda Gabler

HENRY JAMES
Daisy Miller
The Ambassadors
The Europeans
The Portrait of a Lady
The Turn of the Screw
Washington Square

SAMUEL JOHNSON
Rasselas

BEN JONSON
The Alchemist
Volpone

JAMES JOYCE
A Portrait of the Artist as a Young Man
Dubliners

JOHN KEATS
Selected Poems

RUDYARD KIPLING
Kim

D. H. LAWRENCE
Sons and Lovers
The Rainbow
Women in Love

CAMARA LAYE
L'Enfant Noir

HARPER LEE
To Kill a Mocking-Bird

LAURIE LEE
Cider with Rosie

THOMAS MANN
Tonio Kröger

CHRISTOPHER MARLOWE
Doctor Faustus
Edward II

ANDREW MARVELL
Selected Poems

W. SOMERSET MAUGHAM
Of Human Bondage
Selected Short Stories

GAVIN MAXWELL
Ring of Bright Water

J. MEADE FALKNER
Moonfleet

HERMAN MELVILLE
Billy Budd
Moby Dick

THOMAS MIDDLETON
Women Beware Women

THOMAS MIDDLETON and WILLIAM ROWLEY
The Changeling

ARTHUR MILLER
Death of a Salesman
The Crucible

JOHN MILTON
Paradise Lost I & II
Paradise Lost IV & IX
Selected Poems

V. S. NAIPAUL
A House for Mr Biswas

SEAN O'CASEY
Juno and the Paycock
The Shadow of a Gunman

GABRIEL OKARA
The Voice

EUGENE O'NEILL
Mourning Becomes Electra

GEORGE ORWELL
Animal Farm
Nineteen Eighty-four

JOHN OSBORNE
Look Back in Anger

WILFRED OWEN
Selected Poems

ALAN PATON
Cry, The Beloved Country

THOMAS LOVE PEACOCK
Nightmare Abbey and *Crotchet Castle*

HAROLD PINTER
The Birthday Party
The Caretaker

PLATO
The Republic

ALEXANDER POPE
Selected Poems

THOMAS PYNCHON
The Crying of Lot 49

SIR WALTER SCOTT
Ivanhoe
Quentin Durward
The Heart of Midlothian
Waverley

PETER SHAFFER
The Royal Hunt of the Sun

WILLIAM SHAKESPEARE
A Midsummer Night's Dream
Antony and Cleopatra
As You Like It
Coriolanus
Cymbeline
Hamlet
Henry IV Part I
Henry IV Part II
Henry V
Julius Caesar
King Lear
Love's Labour Lost
Macbeth
Measure for Measure
Much Ado About Nothing
Othello
Richard II
Richard III
Romeo and Juliet
Sonnets
The Merchant of Venice
The Taming of the Shrew
The Tempest
The Winter's Tale
Troilus and Cressida
Twelfth Night
The Two Gentlemen of Verona

GEORGE BERNARD SHAW
Androcles and the Lion
Arms and the Man
Caesar and Cleopatra
Candida
Major Barbara
Pygmalion
Saint Joan
The Devil's Disciple

MARY SHELLEY
Frankenstein

PERCY BYSSHE SHELLEY
Selected Poems

RICHARD BRINSLEY SHERIDAN
The School for Scandal
The Rivals

WOLE SOYINKA
The Lion and the Jewel
The Road
Three Shorts Plays

EDMUND SPENSER
The Faerie Queene (Book I)

JOHN STEINBECK
Of Mice and Men
The Grapes of Wrath
The Pearl

LAURENCE STERNE
A Sentimental Journey
Tristram Shandy

ROBERT LOUIS STEVENSON
Kidnapped
Treasure Island
Dr Jekyll and Mr Hyde

TOM STOPPARD
Professional Foul
Rosencrantz and Guildenstern are Dead

JONATHAN SWIFT
Gulliver's Travels

JOHN MILLINGTON SYNGE
The Playboy of the Western World

TENNYSON
Selected Poems

W. M. THACKERAY
Vanity Fair

DYLAN THOMAS
Under Milk Wood

EDWARD THOMAS
Selected Poems

FLORA THOMPSON
Lark Rise to Candleford

J. R. R. TOLKIEN
The Hobbit
The Lord of the Rings

CYRIL TOURNEUR
The Revenger's Tragedy

ANTHONY TROLLOPE
Barchester Towers

MARK TWAIN
Huckleberry Finn
Tom Sawyer

JOHN VANBRUGH
The Relapse

VIRGIL
The Aeneid

VOLTAIRE
Candide

EVELYN WAUGH
Decline and Fall
A Handful of Dust

JOHN WEBSTER
The Duchess of Malfi
The White Devil

H. G. WELLS
The History of Mr Polly
The Invisible Man
The War of the Worlds

ARNOLD WESKER
Chips with Everything
Roots

PATRICK WHITE
Voss

OSCAR WILDE
The Importance of Being Earnest

TENNESSEE WILLIAMS
The Glass Menagerie

VIRGINIA WOOLF
Mrs Dalloway
To the Lighthouse

WILLIAM WORDSWORTH
Selected Poems

WILLIAM WYCHERLEY
The Country Wife

W. B. YEATS
Selected Poems

York Handbooks: list of titles

YORK HANDBOOKS form a companion series to York Notes and are designed to meet the wider needs of students of English and related fields. Each volume is a compact study of a given subject area, written by an authority with experience in communicating the essential ideas to students of all levels.

AN INTRODUCTORY GUIDE TO ENGLISH LITERATURE
by MARTIN STEPHEN

PREPARING FOR EXAMINATIONS IN ENGLISH LITERATURE
by NEIL McEWAN

EFFECTIVE STUDYING
by STEVE ROBERTSON *and* DAVID SMITH

THE ENGLISH NOVEL
by IAN MILLIGAN

ENGLISH POETRY
by CLIVE T. PROBYN

DRAMA: PLAYS, THEATRE AND PERFORMANCE
by MARGERY MORGAN

AN INTRODUCTION TO LINGUISTICS
by LORETO TODD

STUDYING CHAUCER
by ELISABETH BREWER

STUDYING SHAKESPEARE
by MARTIN STEPHEN *and* PHILIP FRANKS

AN A·B·C OF SHAKESPEARE
by P. C. BAYLEY

STUDYING MILTON
by GEOFFREY M. RIDDEN

STUDYING CHARLES DICKENS
by K. J. FIELDING

STUDYING THOMAS HARDY
by LANCE ST JOHN BUTLER

STUDYING THE BRONTËS
by SHEILA SULLIVAN

STUDYING JAMES JOYCE
by HARRY BLAMIRES

ENGLISH LITERATURE FROM THE THIRD WORLD
by TREVOR JAMES

ENGLISH USAGE
by COLIN G. HEY

ENGLISH GRAMMAR
by LORETO TODD

STYLE IN ENGLISH PROSE
by NEIL McEWAN

AN INTRODUCTION TO LITERARY CRITICISM
by RICHARD DUTTON

A DICTIONARY OF LITERARY TERMS
by MARTIN GRAY

READING THE SCREEN
An Introduction to Film Studies
by JOHN IZOD